New Intercessions for the Church Year

A Weekly Companion to ASB

Susan Sayers

First published in 1994 by
KEVIN MAYHEW LTD
Rattlesden
Bury St Edmunds
Suffolk IP30 0SZ

© 1995 Kevin Mayhew Ltd

New Intercessions for the Church Year
is extracted from
Springboard Two

Front cover: *Multi-coloured silk embroidery on white satin,
Chinese textile c. 1850* (detail). Reproduced by courtesy
of the Board of Trustees of the Victoria and
Albert Museum/Bridgeman Art Library, London.

ISBN   0 86209 588 3
Catalogue No 1500015

Cover design by Graham Johnstone
Typesetting and Page Creation by Vicky Brown

**Printed and bound in Great Britain by
J.B.Offset Printers Marks Tey, Colchester, Essex**

Contents

Foreword

A praying church is a living organism, powered by the love of God, and directed by his will. The aim of those leading intercessions in public worship is to provide a suitable climate for prayer, both for the faithful core of praying members, and also for those who drift in as visitors, sometimes willingly and sometimes rather grudgingly.

Since our God is in a far better position to know the needs of each muddle of people who arrive on any particular Sunday, it is obviously sensible to prepare for leading the intercessions by praying for those who will be there, asking our God to lead us with his agenda in mind, rather than taking immediate charge ourselves. Then we have to give him a chance to answer! You may find that a quiet walk enables you to do this, or a time wandering round the empty church, or time spent on some of the mechanical jobs at home while you still your heart and resist the temptation to badger God with good ideas.

I have provided ideas to reflect the theme of the day's readings, and as you read through them you may well find that these ideas will spark off other thoughts of your own. Do use them however you wish – exactly as they stand, adapted to suit specific needs, or simply as a starting point. They are a resource to help you, not a cage to keep your own ideas out.

During the service be alert to what is being said and how God is moving among you, so that you can pick up on these threads, if it seems appropriate, during the intercessions. And if you have young children present, give some thought to how they can also be praying at this time. They might be following a picture prayer trail, singing a quiet worship song, drawing some situation they are praying for or looking through the intercession pictures provided in children's communion books, such as *Jesus is Here* (Kevin Mayhew, 1993).

I have heard it said that, since God can hear the prayers, it doesn't really matter if the congregation can't. I don't agree. In public worship it can be very distracting to be straining to hear, or isolating if you can hear only a vague mumble. Do take the trouble to practise speaking clearly and fairly slowly in the church, so that everyone can comfortably take in what you are saying. Bear in mind that nerves usually make us speed up somewhat, so speak extra slowly to allow for this.

Finally, don't recite what you have written, but pray it. Pray it both through the intentions and through the silences. Leading the intercessions carries a great responsibility, but it is also a great privilege.

SUSAN SAYERS

Some suggestions for opening sentences:

Quietening ourselves in our Father's company,
let us pray together.

As sons and daughters of the Living God,
we come to pray.

Knowing that we are accepted and loved
by the God who made us, let us pray.

Our God is listening;
let us pray to him now.

With love in our hearts for God
and for one another, let us pray.

9th Sunday before Christmas

YEAR 1

This earth is God's earth.

Lord of the earth we stand on,
the air we breathe, the food we grow,
keep us in touch with this planet we inhabit;
help us to tend it well and enjoy its beauty.
Silence for prayer
Lord of heaven and earth:
let your kingdom come

Lord of our past and our future,
Lord of our longings and disappointments,
teach us to recognise you in every moment
and know you are there
through the good and the bad times.
Silence for prayer
Lord of heaven and earth:
let your kingdom come

Lord of our fears and uncertainties,
of our laughter and our foolishness,
fill us with thankfulness
and remind us of how great it is
to be alive.

Silence for prayer

Lord of heaven and earth:
let your kingdom come

Lord of our families and our friends,
of those we like and those we don't;
breathe into our loving
the loving you show to us.

Silence for prayer

Merciful Father,
accept these prayers
for the sake of your Son,
our Saviour Jesus Christ, Amen.

YEAR 2

This earth is God's earth.

We pray for everyone who has never yet
heard of Jesus,
and all those who don't yet know
how much God loves them.
Enable us to use each opportunity
we are given
to show God's love in our behaviour.
Silence for prayer
With God:
nothing is impossible!

We pray for the Queen and those who
govern our country;
we ask you to be among them as they
make important decisions.
We bring to you the many problems
that are so difficult to solve lovingly.
Silence for prayer
With God:
nothing is impossible!

We pray for all who spend their lives
feeling dissatisfied;
for those who are unhappy, lonely or overworked.
We ask you to lift their spirits
and give them peace and joy.
Silence for prayer
With God:
nothing is impossible!

We pray for those in pain
and those whose peaceful lives
have suddenly been shattered.
Help them gather the fragments to start again;
give courage and hope.

Silence for prayer

With God:
nothing is impossible!

Lord, we thank you that your grace
is sufficient for us,
no matter what happens to us.
In a time of silence in God's company,
let us thank him for his many blessings.

Silence for prayer

Merciful Father,
accept these prayers
for the sake of your Son,
our Saviour Jesus Christ, Amen.

8th Sunday
before Christmas

YEAR 1

Sin destroys us; God can save us.

Father, we offer ourselves and our lives to you,
and long for those who do not yet know you
to receive your love with joy.

Silence for prayer

You are the one, true God:
we trust you and adore you

Father, release our grip
on all that prevents us
from living fully in your light;
alert our minds and hearts
to do your will.

Silence for prayer

You are the one, true God:
we trust you and adore you

Father, wherever there is pain or suffering
in our world,
come and save us;
bring good out of every tragedy.

Silence for prayer

You are the one, true God:
we trust you and adore you

Father, we thank you for the refreshment
and encouragement you give us!

Silence for prayer

Merciful Father,
**accept these prayers
for the sake of your Son,
our Saviour Jesus Christ, Amen.**

YEAR 2

Sin destroys us; God can save us.

We pray for all who are fearful
of being themselves;
for those whose lives seem pointless.
Silence for prayer
Lord, we trust in you:
we trust you to respond in love

We pray for those in ordained
and lay ministries;
for a deepening of our own commitment
to Christ.
Silence for prayer
Lord, we trust in you:
we trust you to respond in love

We pray for those who are going through
difficult times at the moment;
those whose lives seem full
of pain and darkness.
Silence for prayer
Lord, we trust in you:
we trust you to respond in love

We thank you for all the special blessings
of our own lives;
for all your patience and gentleness
with us.

Silence for prayer

Merciful Father,
accept these prayers
for the sake of your Son,
our Saviour Jesus Christ, Amen.

7th Sunday before Christmas

YEAR 1

God chooses Abraham;
Abraham responds in faith.

Pray for all who have been chosen as spiritual leaders;
pray for their encouragement and good health,
pray that they stay attentive to God.
Silence for prayer
Teach us, Lord to trust you:
let your will be done

Pray for those setting out on new careers,
or a new phase of life.
Silence for prayer
Teach us, Lord to trust you:
let your will be done

Pray for those whose bodies
don't work as well as they used to;
pray for people to befriend the lonely.
Silence for prayer
Teach us, Lord to trust you:
let your will be done

Pray for the people you would like to spend
more time with,
and those you would be relieved to spend
less time with;
remembering both are loved by God.

Silence for prayer

Teach us, Lord to trust you:
let your will be done

Think of your spiritual journey up to date,
and thank God for the way he is teaching
and guiding you.

Silence for prayer

Merciful Father,
accept these prayers
for the sake of your Son,
our Saviour Jesus Christ, Amen.

YEAR 2

God chooses Abraham;
Abraham responds in faith.

Pray for all those whose faith
is worn or battered,
bringing to mind anyone known to you.
Silence for prayer
For with God:
everything is possible

Pray for a deepening of faith in all church-goers,
particularly those in your own area.
Silence for prayer
For with God:
everything is possible

Pray for our society to be changed and
renewed in God's way, bringing to mind
the areas that particularly concern you.
Silence for prayer
For with God:
everything is possible

Pray for those who are in pain or anguish
and those who are frightened.
Silence for prayer
For with God:
everything is possible

Thank God for what he is doing in your life,
and for his living presence with us
now and always.

Silence for prayer

Merciful Father,
accept these prayers
for the sake of your Son,
our Saviour Jesus Christ, Amen.

6th Sunday
before Christmas

YEAR 1

*God is a rescuer and redeemer
of his people.*

Bring to God's love all who teach the faith
to others;
pray for their work
and their personal life.

Silence for prayer

Father:
let your will be done

Bring to God's affection all who feel
worthless or inadequate.
Pray for their lives to be freed
and transformed.

Silence for prayer

Father:
let your will be done

Bring to God's compassion the areas of war
and violence.
Pray for those caught up in the fighting
and for those trying to negotiate
a just settlement.

Silence for prayer

Father:
let your will be done

Bring to God's peace all the rush and business
of our world.
Pray for a right balance in our lives
between doing and being;
between speaking out and holding our tongues.

Silence for prayer

Father:
let your will be done

Bring your thankfulness to God
for his constant love and faithfulness.

Silence for prayer

Merciful Father,
accept these prayers
for the sake of your Son,
our Saviour Jesus Christ, Amen.

YEAR 2

*God is a rescuer and redeemer
of his people.*

Let us pray together for the leaders
of the churches
and for the spiritual growth
of all Christians.

Silence for prayer

Father, in you we trust:
work your will in our lives

Let us pray for the areas of our world
where there is oppression and violence,
pleading for peace and justice.

Silence for prayer

Father, in you we trust:
work your will in our lives

Let us pray for our home life,
for all the members of our families;
and for those who live
in our neighbourhood.

Silence for prayer

Father, in you we trust:
work your will in our lives

Let us pray for those who feel imprisoned
by bad health or some kind of disability.

Silence for prayer

Father, in you we trust:
work your will in our lives

Let us remember those who have died –
those known personally to us
and those we have heard about –
and pray for all who are torn apart by grief.

Silence for prayer

Father, in you we trust:
work your will in our lives

Let us give thanks for all that is good
and honest, loving and refreshing.

Silence for prayer

Merciful Father,
**accept these prayers
for the sake of your Son,
our Saviour Jesus Christ, Amen.**

5th Sunday
before Christmas

YEAR 1

God preserves a remnant,
whatever the surrounding evil.

Father, we pray through your Spirit
for those who do not know you;
for those who try to control you.
Silence for prayer
Great is our God:
and great is his power

Father, we pray through your Spirit
for a world which is bleeding and aching;
fighting and starving;
cruel and vulnerable.
Silence for prayer
Great is our God:
and great is his power

Father, we pray through your Spirit
for the hurting and hating;
for the damaged and the deluded;
for the ruthless and the wretched.
Silence for prayer
Great is our God:
and great is his power

Father, we pray through your Spirit
for those we love and cherish
and for those we work at loving.

Silence for prayer

Great is our God:
and great is his power

Father, through your Spirit
we thank you for the flow of your love
which fills our lives with colour and joy.

Silence for prayer

Merciful Father,
accept these prayers
for the sake of your Son,
our Saviour Jesus Christ, Amen.

YEAR 2

*God preserves a remnant,
whatever the surrounding evil.*

Father, we come to you
well aware of our habit of selfishness
which distorts your will
and wastes your opportunities;
and yet in trust we can lean on your love.

Silence for prayer

You are our God:
the God who heals and restores us

Father, we come to you
recognising the human weaknesses
of the church
and sorrowful at her divisions;
and yet in anticipation we can lean on your love.

Silence for prayer

You are our God:
the God who heals and restores us

Father, we come to you
wearied and angered by the cruelty
and injustice
of a self-centred world;
and yet in hope we can lean on your love.

Silence for prayer

You are our God:
the God who heals and restores us

Father, we come to you
sharing the pain of all those who suffer,
sharing the grief of all those who mourn;
and yet in peace we can lean on your love.

Silence for prayer

You are our God:
the God who heals and restores us

Father, we come to you
thrilled by your beauty and wisdom and grace;
and filled with your joy we can lean on your love.

Silence for prayer

Merciful Father,
accept these prayers
for the sake of your Son,
our Saviour Jesus Christ, Amen.

1st Sunday in Advent

YEAR 1

*Keep alert, because much is demanded
of those to whom much is entrusted.*

When the pressures of the day
fragment our peace,
keep us watchful and alert,
both for ourselves and for the world.

Silence for prayer

For who is God but the Lord:
who is our rock but our God?

When false values are paraded
among the true,
keep us watchful and alert,
both for ourselves and for our young.

Silence for prayer

For who is God but the Lord:
who is our rock but our God?

When our tight schedules
leave no time for being merely available,
keep us watchful and alert,
both for ourselves and for those who need a listener.

Silence for prayer

For who is God but the Lord:
who is our rock but our God?

When the injustice of the world laughs
at our insignificance,
keep us watchful and alert,
both for ourselves and for all who rely
on our solidarity with them.

Silence for prayer

For who is God but the Lord:
who is our rock but our God?

When we begin to take the wonder of
your creation for granted,
keep us watchful and alert,
both for ourselves and for every person
you cherish.

Silence for prayer

Merciful Father,
accept these prayers
for the sake of your Son,
our Saviour Jesus Christ, Amen.

YEAR 2

*Keep alert, because much is demanded
of those to whom much is entrusted.*

Father, in love we stand alongside
all those who lead and minister
in your church.
We ask you to bless their lives
and their work.
Silence for prayer

God our Father:
we want to walk with you

Father, in love we stand alongside
our Queen and all the leaders of the nations.
We ask you to guide them in your ways.
Silence for prayer

God our Father:
we want to walk with you

Father, in love we stand alongside
all whose lives are bound up with ours.
Work with tenderness in the relationships
we bring before you now.
Silence for prayer

God our Father:
we want to walk with you

Father, in love we stand alongside
all whose bodies, minds or spirits are hurting.
We ask you to minister to them now.

Silence for prayer

God our Father:
we want to walk with you

Father, in love we stand alongside
all who are close to death
and we pray now for your mercy.

Silence for prayer

God our Father:
we want to walk with you

Father, with love in our hearts
we want to thank you
for all you are and all you do in our lives.

Silence for prayer

Merciful Father,
accept these prayers
for the sake of your Son,
our Saviour Jesus Christ, Amen.

2nd Sunday in Advent

YEAR 1

*The Word of God has been gradually
unfolded all through the
Old Testament, throughout
the New Testament and ever since.*

Father, we think of the difficulties facing the church;
and pray for all who minister your love.
Silence for prayer
We believe and proclaim:
Jesus is Lord in every situation

Father, we think of the way our world
is torn apart by war and lack of love.
Silence for prayer
We believe and proclaim:
Jesus is Lord in every situation

Father, we think of those
whose lives are hard and twisted.
Silence for prayer
We believe and proclaim:
Jesus is Lord in every situation

Father, we think of the great pressures
on this generation to abandon your ways,
and of all those who feel lost
and without real value.

Silence for prayer

We believe and proclaim:
Jesus is Lord in every situation

Father, we think of those we find it hard to relate to,
and of those who sometimes find us
difficult to get on with.

Silence for prayer

We believe and proclaim:
Jesus is Lord in every situation

Father, we think of all
who fill our days with love and friendship.

Silence for prayer

Merciful Father,
accept these prayers
for the sake of your Son,
our Saviour Jesus Christ, Amen.

YEAR 2

*The Word of God has been gradually
unfolded all through the
Old Testament, throughout
the New Testament and ever since.*

Father, we pray for everyone who reads the Bible,
and those who could but don't.

Silence for prayer

Open our hearts:
to recognise your will for us

Father, we pray for your guidance
wherever decisions need to be made.

Silence for prayer

Open our hearts:
to recognise your will for us

Father, we pray for peace and unselfishness
in every area of conflict.

Silence for prayer

Open our hearts:
to recognise your will for us

Father, we pray for greater love and forgiveness
in all relationships.

Silence for prayer

Open our hearts:
to recognise your will for us

Father, we pray for your healing and wholeness
in all those who suffer.

Silence for prayer

Open our hearts:
to recognise your will for us

Father, we lift our hearts in love
to praise you and give you thanks.

Silence for prayer

Merciful Father,
accept these prayers
for the sake of your Son,
our Saviour Jesus Christ, Amen.

3rd Sunday in Advent

YEAR 1

*Through his messengers God prepares
the way for salvation.*

Father, into every situation of doubt and despondency
among your followers,
breathe your faithfulness.

Silence for prayer

Prepare us, O Lord:
to walk in your ways

Father, into our strongholds of ambition
and defensiveness,
breathe your humility.

Silence for prayer

Prepare us, O Lord:
to walk in your ways

Father, into the prisons of guilt and revenge,
breathe the grace of forgiveness.

Silence for prayer

Prepare us, O Lord:
to walk in your ways

Father, into the darkness of pain and fear,
breathe your reassurance.

Silence for prayer

Prepare us, O Lord:
to walk in your ways

Father, into the flabbiness of complacency,
breathe your zeal.

Silence for prayer

Prepare us, O Lord:
to walk in your ways

Father, into our homes and places of work,
breathe your fellowship and love.

Silence for prayer

Prepare us, O Lord:
to walk in your ways

Father, into the whole of your creation,
breathe your joy and peace.

Silence for prayer

Merciful Father,
accept these prayers
for the sake of your Son,
our Saviour Jesus Christ, Amen.

YEAR 2

*Through his messengers God prepares
the way for salvation.*

Father, in all areas of weakness
and self-interest in your church,
both as individuals and collectively,
Lord, change us:
from the inside out

Silence for prayer

Father, in all areas of hardened resentment
and desire for revenge among the nations,
Lord, change us:
from the inside out

Silence for prayer

Father, in all areas of discord and misunderstanding
in our relationships with one another,
Lord, change us:
from the inside out

Silence for prayer

Father, in all areas of guilt and regret
which haunt us from our past,
Lord, change us:
from the inside out

Silence for prayer

Father, in the time of our dying;
at the time of your coming in glory,
Lord, change us:
from the inside out

Silence for prayer

Father, enable us to praise you
not only with our lips
but in our lives,
Lord, change us:
from the inside out

Silence for prayer

Merciful Father,
**accept these prayers
for the sake of your Son,
our Saviour Jesus Christ, Amen.**

4th Sunday in Advent

YEAR 1

*After years of waiting,
the Lord is very near.*

Father, we thank you for raising up leaders
and ministers in your church,
and we pray for them now.
Silence for prayer
In your way, Lord:
let your will be done in us

Father, we thank you for all that is good
in our society and pray now for all in
positions of authority.
Silence for prayer
In your way, Lord:
let your will be done in us

Father, we thank you for our homes and families,
for our friends and neighbours.
Silence for prayer
In your way, Lord:
let your will be done in us

Father, we thank you for those who care for the sick,
the distressed and the dying.

Silence for prayer

In your way, Lord:
let your will be done in us

Father, we thank you for all those who worked with you,
in your plan of salvation for us.
Work also in us for the good of your world.

Silence for prayer

Merciful Father,
accept these prayers
for the sake of your Son,
our Saviour Jesus Christ, Amen.

YEAR 2

*After years of waiting,
the Lord is very near.*

Father, we ask for your will to be accomplished
in your church.
Silence for prayer
God in heaven:
let your kingdom come

Father, we plead for mercy
on behalf of a petulant, self-seeking world.
Silence for prayer
God in heaven:
let your kingdom come

Father, we ask your blessing on all who strive
for peace and justice.
Silence for prayer
God in heaven:
let your kingdom come

Father, we welcome your presence
in our families and friendships.
Silence for prayer
God in heaven:
let your kingdom come

Father, we stand in your name
against all that is evil.

Silence for prayer

God in heaven:
let your kingdom come

Father, we ask you to prepare us for the day
when Jesus returns in glory.

Silence for prayer

Merciful Father,
accept these prayers
for the sake of your Son,
our Saviour Jesus Christ, Amen.

Christmas Day

YEARS 1 AND 2

*Jesus Christ is God's good news in
language humankind can understand.*

We pray for all the groups of Christians
who are celebrating your birth today.
Silence for prayer
O God, we thank you:
for loving us so much

We pray for all babies,
that they may be given love and care.
Silence for prayer
O God, we thank you:
for loving us so much

We pray for all who are missing their loved ones,
and all who find Christmas difficult.
Silence for prayer
O God, we thank you:
for loving us so much

We pray for all those in pain
and those with debilitating illness.
Silence for prayer
O God, we thank you:
for loving us so much

We pray for those in prison
and for their families.

Silence for prayer

O God, we thank you:
for loving us so much

We pray for the homeless,
and all refugees.

Silence for prayer

O God, we thank you:
for loving us so much

We thank you for the joy of Christmas
and welcome you in our homes.

Silence for prayer

Merciful Father,
accept these prayers
for the sake of your Son,
our Saviour Jesus Christ, Amen.

1st Sunday after Christmas

YEAR 1

*Laying his glory and majesty aside,
God is content to enter human life as
a vulnerable baby.*

Father, breathe your life
into every worshipping community,
and heal all disunity in your church.
Silence for prayer
God of glory:
we thank you for loving us

Father, breathe your peace into our world
both in individuals and in nations.
Silence for prayer
God of glory:
we thank you for loving us

Father, breathe your joy into our homes
and places of work and leisure.
Silence for prayer
God of glory:
we thank you for loving us

Father, breathe your comfort into all who suffer,
whether mentally, physically,
emotionally or spiritually.

Silence for prayer

God of glory:
we thank you for loving us

Father, breathe your hope into those
who feel they have little to live for.

Silence for prayer

God of glory:
we thank you for loving us

Father, breathe your refreshment and delight
into our attitudes,
until we live in thankfulness.

Silence for prayer

Merciful Father,
accept these prayers
for the sake of your Son,
our Saviour Jesus Christ, Amen.

YEAR 2

*Laying his glory and majesty aside,
God is content to enter human life as
a vulnerable baby.*

Father, we think of the variety of individuals
who make up your church;
make us quick to encourage one another
and slow to criticise.
Silence for prayer
Thank you, Lord:
for restoring us through love

Father, we think of the responsibility we all have
in looking after our world,
and our desperate need for guidance.
Silence for prayer
Thank you, Lord:
for restoring us through love

Father, we think of the joys and sorrows
among families and friends,
and our need of the grace to forgive one another.
Silence for prayer
Thank you, Lord:
for restoring us through love

Father, we think of the pain
which so many suffer all over the world,
and of their thirst for comfort and encouragement.

Silence for prayer

Thank you, Lord:
for restoring us through love

Father, we think of all those who dedicate their lives
to building with you,
and thank you for their faithfulness.

Silence for prayer

Merciful Father,
accept these prayers
for the sake of your Son,
our Saviour Jesus Christ, Amen.

2nd Sunday after Christmas

YEAR 1

*God's salvation is for all peoples and
nations; everyone is eligible.*

Father, into your care we commit all Christians,
all in ministry and all church leaders.
Silence for prayer
O Lord, our God:
it is good to be safe in your love

Father, into your care we commit our world,
with its needs and failures,
hope and despair.
Silence for prayer
O Lord, our God:
it is good to be safe in your love

Father, into your care we commit those we love,
and those we could love more.
Silence for prayer
O Lord, our God:
it is good to be safe in your love

Father, into your care we commit those of all ages
who are in danger,
and live in fear.

Silence for prayer

O Lord, our God:
it is good to be safe in your love

Father, into your care we commit
those who have recently died
and all who mourn for them.

Silence for prayer

O Lord, our God:
it is good to be safe in your love

Father, we rejoice in the way you look after us,
and thank you for providing for all our needs.

Silence for prayer

Merciful Father,
accept these prayers
for the sake of your Son,
our Saviour Jesus Christ, Amen.

YEAR 2

*God's salvation is for all peoples and
nations; everyone is eligible.*

Father, work your love in the church,
her ministers and all her members,
particularly where there is any hardness of heart,
or misunderstanding of your will.

Silence for prayer

Lord, we know and believe:
that you will keep us safe

Father, work your love in our world,
guiding our leaders and redeeming good
from all that is evil.

Silence for prayer

Lord, we know and believe:
that you will keep us safe

Father, work your love in our homes,
making them places of welcome,
understanding and forgiveness.

Silence for prayer

Lord, we know and believe:
that you will keep us safe

Father, work your love in all areas of pain and illness,
anxiety and imprisonment.

Silence for prayer

Lord, we know and believe:
that you will keep us safe

Father, work your love in all areas of sadness
and loneliness,
hopelessness and doubt.

Silence for prayer

Lord, we know and believe:
that you will keep us safe

Father, work your love in all that is beautiful,
all that is growing,
and all that touches our hearts with joy.

Silence for prayer

Merciful Father,
accept these prayers
for the sake of your Son,
our Saviour Jesus Christ, Amen.

Epiphany

YEARS 1 AND 2

*In Jesus we see
God's secret plan revealed.*

We pray for all who spend their lives
leading others to you,
supporting and encouraging them on your journey;
give them your ideas, their love for others,
your joy and your humility.

Silence for prayer

Father, today and every day:
lead us to yourself

We pray for our leaders and advisers in politics,
business, education and health;
for good values, integrity and compassion,
for courage to stand up for what is right.

Silence for prayer

Father, today and every day:
lead us to yourself

We pray for our relationships with our neighbours,
colleagues and those in our family;
for the grace to forgive readily,
listen attentively and to be available
whenever you need us.

Silence for prayer

Father, today and every day:
lead us to yourself

We pray for the frail and the wounded,
the harassed and the despairing;
for hope in suffering, comfort in distress,
and healing of body, mind and spirit.

Silence for prayer

Father, today and every day:
lead us to yourself

We pray for those who have died,
and for those who mourn and miss their company;
we pray for the grace to die a good death
and live with you for ever in the joy of heaven.

Silence for prayer

Father, today and every day:
lead us to yourself

We thank you for all those who have helped
and inspired us on our Christian journey;
for the experiences that have led us
to know and love you more.

Silence for prayer

Merciful Father,
accept these prayers
for the sake of your Son,
our Saviour Jesus Christ, Amen.

1st Sunday after the Epiphany

YEAR 1

*God gives us the grace necessary
to reveal his glory.*

Father, we pray for the church on earth;
wherever your vision is disturbing our assumptions,
wherever your promptings are nudging us to action,
we ask you to keep us attentive and obedient.
Silence for prayer
Give us your grace:
and let your glory shine

Father, we pray for our world;
wherever self interest is blinding us to needs,
wherever past evils are preventing peace,
we ask you to renew us in love.
Silence for prayer
Give us your grace:
and let your glory shine

Father, we pray for our homes and our neighbourhood,
wherever there is a breakdown in communication,
wherever patience wears thin, or interests clash,
we ask for your guidance and protection.
Silence for prayer
Give us your grace:
and let your glory shine

Father, we pray for those who are suffering,
wherever pain or terror is overwhelming,
wherever lives are damaged and wounded,
we ask you to bind up and make whole again.

Silence for prayer

Give us your grace:
and let your glory shine

Father, we pray for the dead and dying,
and those who mourn;
wherever souls are approaching your eternal kingdom,
wherever loved ones grieve,
we ask for your mercy and comfort.

Silence for prayer

Give us your grace:
and let your glory shine

Father, we pray for our hearts to be filled
with thankfulness.
Wherever we see beauty and loveliness,
wherever we experience compassion and forgiveness,
we ask you to lift our hearts to give you glory.

Silence for prayer

Merciful Father,
accept these prayers
for the sake of your Son,
our Saviour Jesus Christ, Amen.

YEAR 2

*God gives us the grace necessary to
reveal his glory.*

Father, we remember the church communities
which are thriving
and those which seem to be dying;
we pray for all in both lay and ordained ministry,
and ask you to breathe new life into us all.

Silence for prayer

God is with us:
he will never let us down

Father, we remember the world's leaders
and all in local and national government;
we pray for your wisdom, sensitivity
and integrity.

Silence for prayer

God is with us:
he will never let us down

Father, we remember those we live, work
and relax with;
we pray for your loving to enrich all our relationships
and your spirit of forgiveness
to become second nature to us.

Silence for prayer

God is with us:
he will never let us down

Father, we remember those whose bodies ache,
whose spirits shudder
and whose memories terrify.
We pray for your healing and wholeness.
Silence for prayer

God is with us:
he will never let us down

Father, we remember with thankfulness
the lives and examples of loved ones who have died.
We commend the dead and dying
to your merciful love.
Silence for prayer

God is with us:
he will never let us down

Father, we offer you our thanks and praise
for the many times you have rescued us
and the many blessings you lavish on us each day.
Silence for prayer

Merciful Father,
accept these prayers
for the sake of your Son,
our Saviour Jesus Christ, Amen.

2nd Sunday after the Epiphany

YEAR 1

*God calls his disciples to spread the
good news of the Kingdom,
whether the people listen or not.*

Father, we want to pray for all who work
to spread the good news of your love,
for all who face insults and danger in the process.
Silence for prayer
In all things, loving God:
let your will be done

Father, we want to pray for our world's leaders,
for all in positions of authority and influence.
Silence for prayer
In all things, loving God:
let your will be done

Father, we want to pray for the people we are fond of,
and those we find it difficult to get on with.
Silence for prayer
In all things, loving God:
let your will be done

Father, we want to pray for those
who feel trapped by illness, oppression,
disability or guilt.

Silence for prayer

In all things, loving God:
let your will be done

Father, we want to pray for your mercy
on those who have died and on those
approaching death.

Silence for prayer

In all things, loving God:
let your will be done

Father, we want to offer you our thanks
for the way you love us and look after us
so patiently and courteously.

Silence for prayer

Merciful Father,
accept these prayers
for the sake of your Son,
our Saviour Jesus Christ, Amen.

YEAR 2

Our God is a God
of wonders,
and it shows.

Father, we pray for all whose Christian ministry
brings hardship and persecution.
Silence for prayer
Keep us safe, O God:
for in you we take refuge

Father, we pray for all in positions of power
and responsibility,
and those negotiating for peace.
Silence for prayer
Keep us safe, O God:
for in you we take refuge

Father, we pray for those amongst whom
we live and work,
for our friends and all whom we value.
Silence for prayer ·
Keep us safe, O God:
for in you we take refuge

Father, we pray for all who feel
overwhelmed with troubles,
and all who are mentally or physically impaired.
Silence for prayer
Keep us safe, O God:
for in you we take refuge

Father, we pray for those who are fearful
or superstitious,
and those who long to believe in your reality.

Silence for prayer

Keep us safe, O God:
for in you we take refuge

Father, we thank you for all you have taught us
and all you are teaching us in our lives
at the moment.

Silence for prayer

Merciful Father,
accept these prayers
for the sake of your Son,
our Saviour Jesus Christ, Amen.

3rd Sunday
after the Epiphany

YEAR 1

*God reveals himself through
signs and wonders.*

Father, wherever your church has become short-sighted,
inattentive or inflexible,
work in your healing love.
Silence for prayer
Lord, awaken us:
to notice your glory

Father, wherever our nations have lost their way,
their sense of human worth or their integrity,
nourish them with your love.
Silence for prayer
Lord, awaken us:
to notice your glory

Father, wherever our relationships are fragmented,
or shallow or offensive to you,
challenge us with your love.
Silence for prayer
Lord, awaken us:
to notice your glory

Father, wherever people are suffering,
whether physically, mentally or emotionally,
comfort them with your love.

Silence for prayer

Lord, awaken us:
to notice your glory

Father, wherever people are fearful of death,
or anxious for the future,
reassure them with your love.

Silence for prayer

Lord, awaken us:
to notice your glory

Father, wherever your will is being fulfilled,
or hearts are learning to trust your love,
we join you in your joy.

Silence for prayer

Merciful Father,
**accept these prayers
for the sake of your Son,
our Saviour Jesus Christ, Amen.**

YEAR 2

*God reveals himself through
signs and wonders.*

Father, we ask for your encouragement and inspiration
in all areas of ministry in the church;
pour out your blessing on all who work
for the spreading of the Kingdom.

Silence for prayer

Living Spirit of God:
you give us life in abundance

Father, we ask for your guidance and protection
in all areas of conflict and confusion;
pour out your wisdom on all who lead.

Silence for prayer

Living Spirit of God:
you give us life in abundance

Father, we ask for your faithful presence
in our homes, and all the homes in this parish;
pour out your spirit of patience and forgiveness
wherever the sparks fly.

Silence for prayer

Living Spirit of God:
you give us life in abundance

Father, we ask for your reassurance and comfort
wherever people are hurting
or crying inside the brave face;
pour out your welcoming love
and give them the peace they crave.

Silence for prayer

Living Spirit of God:
you give us life in abundance

Father, we ask for your firm holding
wherever our journey leads,
and at the time of death, your mercy.

Silence for prayer

Living Spirit of God:
you give us life in abundance

Father, we ask you to accept with joy
our thanks and praise for all you are,
and all you accomplish.

Silence for prayer

Merciful Father,
accept these prayers
for the sake of your Son,
our Saviour Jesus Christ, Amen.

4th Sunday
after the Epiphany

YEAR 1

*God reveals his glory in the way
he rebuilds and restores.*

Father, we remember all those who spend
their lives proclaiming your truth and love;
protect them from danger within and without,
and refresh them in times of weariness.

Silence for prayer

God of tenderness:
you restore our souls

Father, we remember all heads of state,
ambassadors and political advisers;
let your will for our world be accomplished
through the decisions they make.

Silence for prayer

God of tenderness:
you restore our souls

Father, we remember all families where
relationships are strained;
let peace and understanding love
find their way into every room.

Silence for prayer

God of tenderness:
you restore our souls

Father, we remember those whose bodies
do not function effectively,
and those whose bodies are abused;
bring some good from their suffering
and healing to their needs.

Silence for prayer

God of tenderness:
you restore our souls

Father, we remember those who have died
and also their families and friends;
let their sadness be comforted.

Silence for prayer

God of tenderness:
you restore our souls

Father, we remember all the ordinary,
everyday delights which make us smile
and lift our hearts.

Silence for prayer

Merciful Father,
accept these prayers
for the sake of your Son,
our Saviour Jesus Christ, Amen.

YEAR 2

*God reveals his glory in the way
he rebuilds and restores.*

Father, we call to mind all who teach the Christian faith,
all those in training for ministry,
and those preparing for baptism and confirmation;
we ask for the Spirit to guide us into all truth.

Silence for prayer

Our God listens to his children:
our God answers prayer

Father, we call to mind all those involved in education,
those who report world events and comment on them;
we ask for your wisdom and integrity,
your discernment and values.

Silence for prayer

Our God listens to his children:
our God answers prayer

Father, we call to mind those who have influenced
our thinking this week,
those we influence by our words and behaviour;
we ask you to realign our priorities
and give us courage to live your way.

Silence for prayer

Our God listens to his children:
our God answers prayer

Father, we call to mind all who are suffering
in hospitals, bedsits, huts and houses
throughout the world.
We ask you to restore each person to wholeness and joy.
Silence for prayer
Our God listens to his children:
our God answers prayer

Father, we call to mind those who have
reached the end of their earthly life
and are meeting you face to face;
we ask for your mercy on them,
and on those who miss them.
Silence for prayer
Our God listens to his children:
our God answers prayer

Father, we call to mind the many blessings in our lives,
and the ways you reveal yourself to us;
we ask you to deepen our understanding of you,
so that we can love you more and more.
Silence for prayer
Merciful Father,
accept these prayers
for the sake of your Son,
our Saviour Jesus Christ, Amen.

5th Sunday
after the Epiphany

YEARS 1 AND 2

*God's wisdom is that of a living,
powerful creator.*

Father, renew and deepen the faith of your people;
enable us to spread your good news
by our word and our lives.
Silence for prayer
Living God:
we worship you

Father, breathe your peace into the violence
of our world;
we long for your kingdom to come.
Silence for prayer
Living God:
we worship you

Father, refresh and soothe
all our scratchy and worn relationships;
fill our homes with your love.
Silence for prayer
Living God:
we worship you

Father, comfort and reassure
all those who are suffering;
heal them to wholeness.

Silence for prayer

Living God:
we worship you

Father, have mercy on those who draw close to death;
make us all aware of your abiding presence.

Silence for prayer

Living God:
we worship you

Father, awaken us to see again the wonder
and delight of life;
fill us with thankfulness.

Silence for prayer

Merciful Father,
**accept these prayers
for the sake of your Son,
our Saviour Jesus Christ, Amen.**

6th Sunday
after the Epiphany

YEARS 1 AND 2

Jesus' glory is revealed in the parables he tells.

Father, we bring to mind all pastors and ministers
in your holy, world-wide church;
we thank you for them
and want to support them with our love.
Silence for prayer
The life we live:
is your life within us

Father, we call to mind the responsibilities
we share in acting as stewards of your creation;
increase our love and respect for one another,
regardless of nationality or colour.
Silence for prayer
The life we live:
is your life within us

Father, we call to mind those whom we love
and those who love us;
those we tend to criticise and those we admire.
Silence for prayer
The life we live:
is your life within us

Father, we call to mind all those who are feeling weak
or vulnerable;
all those struggling to make sense of their suffering.
Silence for prayer
The life we live:
is your life within us

Father, we call to mind those who grieve
for their loved ones who have died;
we remember those entering heaven.
Silence for prayer
The life we live:
is your life within us

Father, we call to mind your faithful love,
your patience and your mercy.
Silence for prayer
Merciful Father,
accept these prayers
for the sake of your Son,
our Saviour Jesus Christ, Amen.

9th Sunday before Easter

YEAR 1

Jesus teaches us by meeting us in our present situation and guiding us forwards from there.

Father, breathe your spirit of life
into all the members of your church;
keep us open to your word
and sensitive to your will.

Silence for prayer

All-knowing God:
teach us your ways

Father, breathe your spirit of counsel
into every debate and international conference;
alert us to act with responsibility and integrity.

Silence for prayer

All-knowing God:
teach us your ways

Father, breathe your spirit of love
into every home and neighbourhood;
make us slow to criticise and quick to forgive.

Silence for prayer

All-knowing God:
teach us your ways

Father, breathe your spirit of healing
into all those who are weakened or damaged,
whether physically, mentally, emotionally or spiritually;
give them the reassurance of your presence.

Silence for prayer

All-knowing God:
teach us your ways

Father, breathe your spirit of peace
into those who are approaching death
and those who have recently died.
Help us to trust in your infinite mercy.

Silence for prayer

All-knowing God:
teach us your ways

Father, breathe your spirit of thankfulness
into our hearts as we receive,
our minds as we notice,
and our lives as we journey.

Silence for prayer

Merciful Father,
accept these prayers
for the sake of your Son,
our Saviour Jesus Christ, Amen.

YEAR 2

*Jesus teaches us by meeting us in our
present situation and guiding us
forwards from there.*

Father, we call to mind all those in Christian ministry
and all whom they serve in your strength.
Silence for prayer
Father, we need you:
we depend on you for everything

We call to mind all those who make decisions
which affect our lives
and the life of our planet.
Silence for prayer
Father, we need you:
we depend on you for everything

We call to mind the members of our families
and also our neighbours and friends.
Silence for prayer
Father, we need you:
we depend on you for everything

We call to mind those who are ill
and those who cannot be physically independent.
Silence for prayer
Father, we need you:
we depend on you for everything

We call to mind all who are celebrating
and rejoicing today.
With them we lift our hearts in thankfulness.

Silence for prayer

Merciful Father,
**accept these prayers
for the sake of your Son,
our Saviour Jesus Christ, Amen.**

8th Sunday before Easter

YEAR 1

God knows us inside out.

Father, we bring to your healing love
our shallowness of faith,
our need for your grace and power
in the church throughout the world.
Silence for prayer
You know us completely:
and love us for ever

We bring to your healing love
our need for your serenity and wisdom
in the governments of all the nations.
Silence for prayer
You know us completely:
and love us for ever

We bring to your healing love
our need of patience, mutual affection
and forgiveness
in our homes and families.
Silence for prayer
You know us completely:
and love us for ever

We bring to your healing love
the injured and broken-hearted,
the weak and the frightened.

Silence for prayer

You know us completely:
and love us for ever

We bring to your healing love
those whom death has released from pain,
and those in great sorrow at losing loved ones.

Silence for prayer

You know us completely:
and love us for ever

We bring you our thanks and praise
for all that is good and hopeful and positive,
all that is redeemed from suffering.

Silence for prayer

Merciful Father,
accept these prayers
for the sake of your Son,
our Saviour Jesus Christ, Amen.

YEAR 2

Christ can heal us to wholeness,
but only if we let him.

Father, we bring to you
our desire to see you more clearly.
Silence for prayer
Open our eyes, Lord:
heal us from blindness

Father, we grieve with the oppressed
and downtrodden,
and long for your governing of the nations.
Silence for prayer
Open our eyes, Lord:
heal us from blindness

Father, we lay before you all our relationships,
both the fulfilling and the challenging.
Silence for prayer
Open our eyes, Lord:
heal us from blindness

Father, we remember with affection and love
all those who are in pain or distress,
offering our availability for you to use.
Silence for prayer
Open our eyes, Lord:
heal us from blindness

Father, we call to mind those whom death
has hidden from our eyes,
but whom we continue to love and cherish,
knowing they are safe in your care.

Silence for prayer

Open our eyes, Lord:
heal us from blindness

Father, we thank you
for the gift of physical sight
and the richness of spiritual insight.

Silence for prayer

Merciful Father,
**accept these prayers
for the sake of your Son,
our Saviour Jesus Christ, Amen.**

7th Sunday
before Easter

YEAR 1

*If you are a sinner,
then Jesus considers
you a friend.*

Father, we remember all those who are
insulted or despised for their faith in you.
Silence for prayer
Lord, we take refuge:
in the shadow of your wings

We remember those caught up in conflict,
and those who strive for peace.
Silence for prayer
Lord, we take refuge:
in the shadow of your wings

We remember those who irritate and annoy us,
and those we irritate and annoy.
Silence for prayer
Lord, we take refuge:
in the shadow of your wings

We remember those whose bodies are trapped in pain,
and those whose minds are trapped in confusion.

Silence for prayer

Lord, we take refuge:
in the shadow of your wings

We remember those who have died
and those who ache with mourning.

Silence for prayer

Lord, we take refuge:
in the shadow of your wings

We thank and praise you, O God,
for your parenting and special love for each of us.

Silence for prayer

Merciful Father,
accept these prayers
for the sake of your Son,
our Saviour Jesus Christ, Amen.

YEAR 2

If you are a sinner,
then Jesus considers you a friend.

Father, wherever people's faith is stunted or withered,
we plead for your breath of life.
Silence for prayer
Lord of power:
you can transform our lives

Wherever people are trapped by oppression
or weakened by complacency,
we plead for your kingdom to come.
Silence for prayer
Lord of power:
you can transform our lives

Wherever people live out their daily lives
in stress and disappointment,
we plead for your restoring love.
Silence for prayer
Lord of power:
you can transform our lives

Wherever people's lives are restricted by
physical weakness or hunger or poverty,
we plead for your healing love.
Silence for prayer
Lord of power:
you can transform our lives

Wherever people are dying,
we plead for your mercy and comfort.

Silence for prayer

Lord of power:
you can transform our lives

Wherever there is loveliness and serenity,
integrity and wisdom,
we praise you for your glory.

Silence for prayer

Merciful Father,
accept these prayers
for the sake of your Son,
our Saviour Jesus Christ, Amen.

1st Sunday in Lent

YEAR 1

*We need to build up our defences
against temptation.*

Father, we pray for all who are going through
a time of temptation at the moment.
Strengthen and protect them all.
Silence for prayer

Your commands, O Lord:
are our delight

We pray that your church may always
hold true to your truth and love
with your love.
Silence for prayer

Your commands, O Lord:
are our delight

We pray for those in positions of power
that they may not give way to corruption
but work with integrity.
Silence for prayer

Your commands, O Lord:
are our delight

We pray for those in our families
and those who live in our neighbourhood,
that we may live in harmony together.

Silence for prayer

Your commands, O Lord:
are our delight

We pray for those in prison
and those imprisoned by guilt.

Silence for prayer

Your commands, O Lord:
are our delight

We pray for those who have died through neglect,
mismanagement of resources,
violence and oppression.

Silence for prayer

Your commands, O Lord:
are our delight

Father, we thank you for the way
you protect and enfold us every moment
of every day.

Silence for prayer

Merciful Father,
accept these prayers
for the sake of your Son,
our Saviour Jesus Christ, Amen.

YEAR 2

*We need to build up our defences
against temptation.*

Father, we pray for the church
and all Christians in their various callings;
we remember the conflicts and divisions,
and the movement towards unity.

Silence for prayer

Lord, we believe:
that in all things you work for our good

We pray for those who have been given
great responsibility in this world.

Silence for prayer

Lord, we believe:
that in all things you work for our good

We pray for our parents
and all who have influenced our thinking.

Silence for prayer

Lord, we believe:
that in all things you work for our good

We pray for those in great need,
financially, emotionally or physically.

Silence for prayer

Lord, we believe:
that in all things you work for our good

We pray for those whose earthly journey
has come to an end;
and we pray for those who feel empty
without their physical company.

Silence for prayer

Lord, we believe:
that in all things you work for our good

We praise and thank you, Father,
that we can trust you with our lives.

Silence for prayer

Merciful Father,
accept these prayers
for the sake of your Son,
our Saviour Jesus Christ, Amen.

2nd Sunday in Lent

YEAR 1

Following Christ is not always a comfortable place to be.

We call to mind all who are insulted
or persecuted for their faith;
all who speak out
and those who are afraid to.

Silence for prayer

Help us, O Lord:
we put our trust in you

We call to mind those working for peace,
justice and hope in an aching world.

Silence for prayer

Help us, O Lord:
we put our trust in you

We call to mind those whose lives
are bound up with ours;
we remember all the families and streets
represented here.

Silence for prayer

Help us, O Lord:
we put our trust in you

We call to mind those whose bodies
battle against disease or pain;
those whose minds battle against confusion
and depression.

Silence for prayer

Help us, O Lord:
we put our trust in you

We call to mind those who are dying
in fear or loneliness;
those who have recently passed into eternity.

Silence for prayer

Help us, O Lord:
we put our trust in you

We call to mind the ways we have been helped
through difficult times,
and have grown to understand more
of your loving care.
And we commend the rest of our life to your keeping.

Silence for prayer

Merciful Father,
accept these prayers
for the sake of your Son,
our Saviour Jesus Christ, Amen.

YEAR 2

*Following Christ is not always a
comfortable place to be.*

In the muddle of our ecclesiastical arguments,
our narrow self-interest and our embarrassment,
teach us to fix our eyes on you.

Silence for prayer

Lord, wherever you lead us:
we will go

In our defensiveness and nationalism,
and our fear of being considered weak,
teach us true courage to speak out
for what is right.

Silence for prayer

Lord, wherever you lead us:
we will go

In the comfort of our homes and families,
teach us the grace to be hospitable and welcoming.

Silence for prayer

Lord, wherever you lead us:
we will go

In the needs of those who are ill and injured,
teach us to see your face.

Silence for prayer

Lord, wherever you lead us:
we will go

In the sorrow of dying,
teach us to see also the gateway to heaven.

Silence for prayer

Lord, wherever you lead us:
we will go

In all the beauty of your creation,
teach us to see the beauty of your holiness,
and sing your praise with joy.

Silence for prayer

Merciful Father,
accept these prayers
for the sake of your Son,
our Saviour Jesus Christ, Amen.

3rd Sunday
in Lent

YEAR 1

*Christ had to suffer in order
to rescue us.*

Father, we lean on your love as we pray
for your church – collectively,
and as a mixed bag of individuals,
with needs, disappointments and fears.

Silence for prayer

In all things, Father:
we pray your kingdom in

We lean on your wisdom as we pray
for local, national and international leaders,
subject to pressures and conflicting values.

Silence for prayer

In all things, Father:
we pray your kingdom in

We lean on your affectionate understanding
as we pray for our homes and all homes in this area,
with their expectations and misunderstandings,
their security and insecurity.

Silence for prayer

In all things, Father:
we pray your kingdom in

We lean on your compassion as we pray
for all who are hurting in body, mind or spirit.

Silence for prayer

In all things, Father:
we pray your kingdom in

We lean on your faithfulness as we pray
for those who have died, and those who mourn.

Silence for prayer

In all things, Father:
we pray your kingdom in

We lean on your accepting love as we pray
in thankfulness for all you are doing in our lives,
and all you have in mind for us in the future.

Silence for prayer

Merciful Father,
**accept these prayers
for the sake of your Son,
our Saviour Jesus Christ, Amen.**

YEAR 2

*Christ had to suffer in order
to rescue us.*

Father, we pray for the church,
your body on earth, with its richness of variety
and its poverty of splits and schisms.
Silence for prayer
You hold our lives:
safe in the palm of your hand

Father, we pray for the world you have created,
with its struggles for peace
and its cravings for fulfilment.
Silence for prayer
You hold our lives:
safe in the palm of your hand

Father, we pray for this neighbourhood
in which you have placed us,
with its visible activity
and its hidden problems.
Silence for prayer
You hold our lives:
safe in the palm of your hand

Father, we pray for those who are ill at home
or in hospital,
with their longing for health
and their struggle with pain.

Silence for prayer

You hold our lives:
safe in the palm of your hand

We pray for the dead and dying,
with their need for mercy
and their hope of heaven.

Silence for prayer

You hold our lives:
safe in the palm of your hand

We pray with thankfulness and love
for the Spirit transforming our lives.

Silence for prayer

Merciful Father,
accept these prayers
for the sake of your Son,
our Saviour Jesus Christ, Amen.

4th Sunday in Lent

YEAR 1

*In the glory of God's presence the covenant
of the law is sealed between God and his people;
Jesus himself becomes the sacrifice binding
them in the new covenant.*

When following you brings danger, Lord,
or weariness or discomfort,
we long for your help.
Silence for prayer
In the shadow of your wings:
we shall be in safety

When we watch the violence and selfishness
of this world,
its bewilderment and fear,
we long for your peace.
Silence for prayer
In the shadow of your wings:
we shall be in safety

When we work through our relationships
and feel for those we love,
we long for your guidance.
Silence for prayer
In the shadow of your wings:
we shall be in safety

When our hearts touch those who suffer,
and know their pain and distress,
we long for your healing love.

Silence for prayer

In the shadow of your wings:
we shall be in safety

When those we love meet death
and we must let them go,
we long for your mercy and welcome.

Silence for prayer

In the shadow of your wings:
we shall be in safety

When we see the beauty and wonder
of your glorious creation and of your holiness,
we long for an eternity to praise you.

Silence for prayer

Merciful Father,
accept these prayers
for the sake of your Son,
our Saviour Jesus Christ, Amen.

YEAR 2

*In the glory of God's presence the covenant
of the law is sealed between God and his people;
Jesus himself becomes the sacrifice binding
them in the new covenant.*

Father, you know us better than we know ourselves,
and are well aware of the needs and pains
in your church.
We lift them now to your healing love.

Silence for prayer

Father, we love you:
we love you and we trust you

In our world there are decisions to be made,
countries to be governed and people to be honoured.
We lift them now to your grace and wisdom.

Silence for prayer

Father, we love you:
we love you and we trust you

In our neighbourhood and in our homes
there are celebrations and tragedies,
times of hope, of weariness and tenderness.
We lift them now to your parenting.

Silence for prayer

Father, we love you:
we love you and we trust you

In our hospitals and clinics there are many in pain,
many who are fearful,
and many who have lost hope.
We lift them now to your comfort and protection.

Silence for prayer

Father, we love you:
we love you and we trust you

As each day others die and enter your presence,
we ask for your mercy
and commend them to your safe keeping.

Silence for prayer

Father, we love you:
we love you and we trust you

As we walk through our lives in your company,
we rejoice in your friendship
and delight in your love for us.

Silence for prayer

Merciful Father,
accept these prayers
for the sake of your Son,
our Saviour Jesus Christ, Amen.

5th Sunday in Lent

YEAR 1

Jesus could only buy us full life by submitting to full death.

Father, we pray for all who follow Christ,
for those whose faith is being tested,
and for those who have drifted away.
Silence for prayer
Into your hands, O Lord:
we place our lives

We pray for all leaders and advisers,
all meetings and councils,
that right decisions may be made.
Silence for prayer
Into your hands, O Lord:
we place our lives

We pray for all those we love
and those we find it difficult to love;
for those whose loving is damaged
and those who have no one who cares about them.
Silence for prayer
Into your hands, O Lord:
we place our lives

We pray for those who are persecuted or imprisoned,
for those locked in fear or hatred
and all who are in need of healing.

Silence for prayer

Into your hands, O Lord:
we place our lives

We pray for those who have died alone or in fear,
for those who are finding it hard to accept
another's death.

Silence for prayer

Into your hands, O Lord:
we place our lives

We give you thanks and praise
for bringing us safely to this moment,
and offer you the future, with all that it holds.

Silence for prayer

Merciful Father,
accept these prayers
for the sake of your Son,
our Saviour Jesus Christ, Amen.

YEAR 2

*Jesus could only buy us full life by
submitting to full death.*

Father, we pray for all in your church
whose journey through life
is hard, dangerous, exhausting or confused.
Silence for prayer
Lord of love:
live and work in us all

We pray for those whose lives are disrupted
by war, famine or political unrest.
Silence for prayer
Lord of love:
live and work in us all

We pray for our families, friends and neighbours,
all who cause us concern
and all in need of your peace.
Silence for prayer
Lord of love:
live and work in us all

We pray for all whose lives are filled
with pain, resentment or hatred,
all trapped in addiction or despair.
Silence for prayer
Lord of love:
live and work in us all

We pray for those who have died,
and those who miss them.

Silence for prayer

Lord of love:
live and work in us all

We give you thanks for the gift of life,
for every moment of every day.

Silence for prayer

Merciful Father,
accept these prayers
for the sake of your Son,
our Saviour Jesus Christ, Amen.

Palm Sunday

YEARS 1 AND 2

*The King of glory rides on a donkey
into Jerusalem.*

We pray for the church, the body of Christ,
longing for its healing, strengthening
and openness to your will.

Silence for prayer

The Lord is among us:
his Spirit prays through ours

We pray for the world and all the nations,
longing for peace and tranquillity,
justice, mercy and forgiveness.

Silence for prayer

The Lord is among us:
his Spirit prays through ours

We pray for all our relatives
and the family life of our country,
longing for the grace to love and honour
one another,
to trust and to persevere.

Silence for prayer

The Lord is among us:
his Spirit prays through ours

We pray for those who are ill or in distress,
longing for your comfort, healing and refreshment.

Silence for prayer

The Lord is among us:
his Spirit prays through ours

We pray for those who are passing
through the gate of death,
longing for your merciful love.

Silence for prayer

The Lord is among us:
his Spirit prays through ours

We praise you and worship you
for all your blessings,
but especially for your generous saving love
and faithful presence with us.

Silence for prayer

Merciful Father,
accept these prayers
for the sake of your Son,
our Saviour Jesus Christ, Amen.

Easter Day

YEARS 1 AND 2

Death cannot hold the Lord of life.
New life for him means new life for all
who believe in Christ.

We think of the church celebrating in clusters
and crowds all over the world,
and pray for a deepening of love and faith.
Silence for prayer
Lord of life:
you do all things well

We remember the areas of the world
where there is conflict and confusion;
and we pray that all may come to know God's love.
Silence for prayer
Lord of life:
you do all things well

We remember those we have met and talked with
during the week,
and pray for God's blessing on their lives.
Silence for prayer
Lord of life:
you do all things well

We remember those waiting for surgery,
and those in long-term care,
and pray that God's will
may be beautifully accomplished in their lives.

Silence for prayer

Lord of life:
you do all things well

We remember those who have died very young,
and those who are finding this hard to accept,
and we pray for God's grace and reassurance.

Silence for prayer

Lord of life:
you do all things well

We remember the wonder and generosity of God,
his faithfulness and his mercy.

Silence for prayer

Merciful Father,
accept these prayers
for the sake of your Son,
our Saviour Jesus Christ, Amen.

1st Sunday after Easter

YEAR 1

In Jesus we see the face of God,
and his risen life enables him to live in us.

We pray for all whose faith is shaky,
those who hesitate to trust you
and those who are just beginning to believe.
Silence for prayer
Open our eyes, Lord:
to know and love you more

We pray for the areas of fighting and bitterness,
for the downtrodden and despised,
for those with authority to improve conditions.
Silence for prayer
Open our eyes, Lord:
to know and love you more

We pray for the very young and the very old,
for mothers, fathers and children
and all the homes in this parish.
Silence for prayer
Open our eyes, Lord:
to know and love you more

We pray for the ill and injured,
those who live fearful, anxious lives
and those who are disillusioned with life.

Silence for prayer

Open our eyes, Lord:
to know and love you more

We pray for those who are approaching death,
those who have died recently
and all who fear death.

Silence for prayer

Open our eyes, Lord:
to know and love you more

We pray for a deeper sense of thankfulness
for all you have given us
and for all you are in us.

Silence for prayer

Merciful Father,
accept these prayers
for the sake of your Son,
our Saviour Jesus Christ, Amen.

YEAR 2

Whatever may happen to us,
ultimately we shall be safe in the hands
of the living God.

When we want to hide from serving you,
when we doubt your promise to be with us,
Lord, teach us:
how to be faithful
Silence for prayer

When we find ourselves standing
against worldly values,
Lord, teach us:
how to be faithful
Silence for prayer

When we meet with selfishness, laziness and criticism
in ourselves and others around us,
Lord, teach us:
how to be faithful
Silence for prayer

When we hear of the ill and lonely who
would welcome some friendly contact,
Lord, teach us:
how to be faithful
Silence for prayer

When we see others die
and remember that this life will pass,
Lord, teach us:
how to be faithful

Silence for prayer

When we grumble and complain
instead of living thankfully,
Lord, teach us:
how to be faithful

Silence for prayer

Merciful Father,
accept these prayers
for the sake of your Son,
our Saviour Jesus Christ, Amen.

2nd Sunday after Easter

YEAR 1

'I bring life'

Wherever Christians are spiritually dry or brittle,
wherever the loving has lost its freshness,
we pray for refreshment.

Silence for prayer

Father, touch our lives:
and give them new life

Wherever the nations scramble for power and revenge,
wherever materialism dulls the spirit,
we pray for realigned priorities and values.

Silence for prayer

Father, touch our lives:
and give them new life

Wherever homes are disturbed by financial problems,
difficult relationships and long-term illness,
we pray for guidance and support.

Silence for prayer

Father, touch our lives:
and give them new life

Wherever slow recovery makes time hang heavily,
wherever hope and joy are fading,
we pray for encouragement and delight.

Silence for prayer

Father, touch our lives:
and give them new life

Wherever people are dying to this world,
wherever lives are cut short by accidents, war or famine,
we pray for your mercy and words of comfort.

Silence for prayer

Father, touch our lives:
and give them new life

Whether our hearts are light or heavy,
whether the day goes well or not,
we give you praise and proclaim your love.

Silence for prayer

Merciful Father,
accept these prayers
for the sake of your Son,
our Saviour Jesus Christ, Amen.

YEAR 2

'I bring life'

We remember the bickering and petty-mindedness
that goes on in all areas of church life,
and ask for your healing love.
Silence for prayer
Show up our darkness:
and cancel it with your light

We remember the bitterness and greed
which tears our world apart,
and ask for your peace.
Silence for prayer
Show up our darkness:
and cancel it with your light

We remember our families, and the homes
in this parish,
with their laughter and crying, anger and frustration,
and ask for your caring love.
Silence for prayer
Show up our darkness:
and cancel it with your light

We remember those who suffer
and find life hard to cope with,
and ask for your comfort and encouragement.
Silence for prayer
Show up our darkness:
and cancel it with your light

We remember those who are moving
from this life into eternity,
and those heartbroken at their going.
We ask for greater trust in you.

Silence for prayer

Show up our darkness:
and cancel it with your light

We thank you and give you glory
for all you are doing in our lives,
and all you have in mind for the future.

Silence for prayer

Merciful Father,
accept these prayers
for the sake of your Son,
our Saviour Jesus Christ, Amen.

3rd Sunday after Easter

YEAR 1

*Even if people don't believe in God,
he never for a moment stops
believing in them.*

Lord of glory, we ask you to show us
more of yourself,
to inspire all ministers and teachers of your word,
freshen our faith and cultivate our love.

Silence for prayer

Our help comes from the Lord:
who has made heaven and earth

Lord of glory, we ask your help in the governing
of our planet,
in all national and international decisions
and in the organisation of our resources.

Silence for prayer

Our help comes from the Lord:
who has made heaven and earth

Lord of glory, we ask you to bring
healing and reassurance, comfort and wholeness
to all who suffer.

Silence for prayer

Our help comes from the Lord:
who has made heaven and earth

Lord of glory, we ask you to welcome
into your presence
those who have reached the point of physical death.

Silence for prayer

Our help comes from the Lord:
who has made heaven and earth

Lord of glory, we give you thanks and praise
for all that is good and lovely,
honest and pure.

Silence for prayer

Merciful Father,
accept these prayers
for the sake of your Son,
our Saviour Jesus Christ, Amen.

YEAR 2

No matter how ruined or damaged our lives are,
God has plans for a full restoration programme
and is ready to start work straight away.

There are places where the church is weak
and complacent; where we are deaf
and blind to where and how you are leading us.
Open our hearts to hear and see you more clearly.

Silence for prayer

Father, let our lives:
be strongly built on your love

There are places where brutal force and corruption
seem to have the upper hand.
Quieten our lives and give space to all leaders
to hear your wisdom.

Silence for prayer

Father, let our lives:
be strongly built on your love

There are homes where arguments flare up
all the time, and people are sad and lonely.
Fill each home in this parish with peace and love.

Silence for prayer

Father, let our lives:
be strongly built on your love

There are people with raging temperatures
and bodies full of pain.
Keep them safe and bring them to wholeness.

Silence for prayer

Father, let our lives:
be strongly built on your love

There are people from every country
who have recently died.
Welcome them into your kingdom
and comfort those who miss them.

Silence for prayer

Father, let our lives:
be strongly built on your love

The world you have given us to live in
is full of beauty.
We thank you for all that fills us with joy.

Silence for prayer

Merciful Father,
accept these prayers
for the sake of your Son,
our Saviour Jesus Christ, Amen.

4th Sunday after Easter

YEAR 1

*Prophets say what we need to hear –
not what we want to hear.*

When we are teased or laughed at
for what we believe;
when we find it hard to be faithful,
then we take refuge:
in the shadow of your wings
Silence for prayer

When we are confronted with violence,
homelessness and war,
and stand alongside the victims and outcasts,
then we take refuge:
in the shadow of your wings
Silence for prayer

When we remember our homes,
and those we live near,
and plead for those who do not know
what it is to be loved,
then we take refuge:
in the shadow of your wings
Silence for prayer

When we are ill or in pain,
anxious or fearful,
then we take refuge:
in the shadow of your wings

Silence for prayer

When we approach death;
when we mourn the loss of loved ones,
then we take refuge:
in the shadow of your wings

Silence for prayer

When we delight in the freshness of creation;
when we feel your joy uplifting us,
then we take refuge:
in the shadow of your wings

Silence for prayer

Merciful Father,
**accept these prayers
for the sake of your Son,
our Saviour Jesus Christ, Amen**

YEAR 2

God not only shows us the route,
but walks with us each step of the way.

Trusting in your love we pray
for all arguments and conflicts in the church;
for all who feel confused about their faith.

Silence for prayer

Father, you hold our lives:
safe in your hands

Trusting in your authority we pray
for all international discussions and negotiations;
for all who give orders to others.

Silence for prayer

Father, you hold our lives:
safe in your hands

Trusting in your gentleness we pray
for new-born children and their parents;
for all families in crisis.

Silence for prayer

Father, you hold our lives:
safe in your hands

Trusting in your wisdom we pray
for those who labour to find cures
and protection from disease;
for all who suffer in body, mind or spirit.

Silence for prayer

Father, you hold our lives:
safe in your hands

Trusting in your mercy we pray
for those who have reached physical death;
for those who miss them or feel guilty about them.

Silence for prayer

Father, you hold our lives:
safe in your hands

Trusting in your goodness we pray
with thankfulness for all we have received
and been enabled to share.

Silence for prayer

Merciful Father,
accept these prayers
for the sake of your Son,
our Saviour Jesus Christ, Amen.

5th Sunday after Easter

YEAR 1

God is far more ready to lavish his blessings on us than we are to receive them.

We remember all the Christians worshipping
all over the world;
especially those who are feeling discouraged
or inadequate.

Silence for prayer

In all your people, Father:
let your will be done

We remember the leaders of the nations,
all in charge of making important decisions
and all who have sidled into corruption.

Silence for prayer

In all your people, Father:
let your will be done

We remember the members of our families
and those who make life easy or difficult for us.

Silence for prayer

In all your people, Father:
let your will be done

We remember those dependent on drugs or alcohol;
all whose bodies don't work properly
and all who have been damaged by violence.

Silence for prayer

In all your people, Father:
let your will be done

We remember those who have died
and those who miss their company.

Silence for prayer

In all your people, Father:
let your will be done

As we delight in the rich variety of your creation,
we offer our lives for you to use
in whatever way you want.

Silence for prayer

Merciful Father,
**accept these prayers
for the sake of your Son,
our Saviour Jesus Christ, Amen.**

YEAR 2

God knows best.

Father, we pray for the excited new Christians
and the mellow, experienced ones;
for the doubting, cynical ones
and the hesitant believers.

Silence for prayer

In every situation:
God knows best

Father, we pray for the responsible
and the peacemakers in our world,
and for the defensive, arrogant and ambitious.

Silence for prayer

In every situation:
God knows best

Father, we pray for the contented, thriving families
and for those struggling to survive each day.

Silence for prayer

In every situation:
God knows best

Father, we pray for those recovering from surgery
and for all those in great pain.

Silence for prayer

In every situation:
God knows best

Father, we pray for those who have recently died
and for those dying now.

Silence for prayer

In every situation:
God knows best

Father, we thank you and praise you
for all the blessings you shower on our lives,
and ask you to keep us in closer touch
with you from now on.

Silence for prayer

Merciful Father,
**accept these prayers
for the sake of your Son,
our Saviour Jesus Christ, Amen.**

Ascension Day and Sunday after Ascension

YEAR 1

*Having paid for our freedom with his life,
Jesus our Saviour enters into the full glory
to which he is entitled.*

Loving Father, give encouragement,
vision and deeper faith to all your followers,
so that the church truly expresses your love.
Silence for prayer
You are our God:
with you, nothing is impossible

Dissolve away all fear, suspicion and greed
which lead to corruption in our world.
Silence for prayer
You are our God:
with you, nothing is impossible

Be present in every home,
so that the love increases
and each person is given respect and value.
Silence for prayer
You are our God:
with you, nothing is impossible

Guide those in medical research
and bring wholeness to all who are in any
way distressed.

Silence for prayer

You are our God:
with you, nothing is impossible

Welcome into your heaven all those at the
stage of death,
and give consolation to their loved ones.

Silence for prayer

You are our God:
with you, nothing is impossible

Give us a greater sense of your glory
so that we can worship you
with our whole being.

Silence for prayer

Merciful Father,
**accept these prayers
for the sake of your Son,
our Saviour Jesus Christ, Amen.**

YEAR 2

*Christ's amazing humility is to be
our perfect example.*

In every church, in every Christian,
we long for God's love to blossom.
Silence for prayer
Amen:
let your glorious will be done

In every country, in everyone
who has influence and authority,
we long for God's wisdom to prevail.
Silence for prayer
Amen:
let your glorious will be done

In every home, in every neighbourhood,
we long for God's forgiveness to flourish.
Silence for prayer
Amen:
let your glorious will be done

In every hospital, in every suffering person,
we long for God's healing to comfort and restore.
Silence for prayer
Amen:
let your glorious will be done

In everyone who mourns, in all who are dying,
we long for God's peace to come.

Silence for prayer

Amen:
let your glorious will be done

In all our joys, our sorrows and our choices,
we rejoice that God is indeed in control.

Silence for prayer

Merciful Father,
accept these prayers
for the sake of your Son,
our Saviour Jesus Christ, Amen.

Pentecost

YEARS 1 AND 2

*When God's Spirit is poured out on
his people, it shows.*

As we still our bodies and open ourselves to God
we think of the church leaders, preachers
and all who minister to God's people.
With them and for them we pray . . .
Silence for prayer
Spirit of the living God:
fall afresh on us

We think of all the world's nations,
the problems, quarrels, misunderstandings
and mistakes.
With them and for them we pray . . .
Silence for prayer
Spirit of the living God:
fall afresh on us

We think of those in our family,
those we like and those we seem to annoy.
With them and for them we pray . . .
Silence for prayer
Spirit of the living God:
fall afresh on us

We think of those in hospitals and hospices,
outpatients at the local accident centre
and those ill at home.
With them and for them we pray . . .

Silence for prayer

Spirit of the living God:
fall afresh on us

We think of those who are close to death,
those who have recently died
and those who miss them.
With them and for them we pray . . .

Silence for prayer

Spirit of the living God:
fall afresh on us

We think of all your amazing creation,
from the microscopic to the cosmic,
and remember with thankfulness that we are part
of this glory you have made.

Silence for prayer

Merciful Father,
accept these prayers
for the sake of your Son,
our Saviour Jesus Christ, Amen.

Trinity Sunday

YEARS 1 AND 2

God is creator, redeemer and life-giver
all at once, in every situation.

Holy God, we come to plead for the church
in its weakness and lack of unity;
may we be one as you are one.
Silence for prayer
Holy God:
we trust in your goodness

Holy God, we come to plead for our world
in its confusion and injustices.
Silence for prayer
Holy God:
we trust in your goodness

Holy God, we come to plead for our families
and friends
in their needs and difficulties.
Silence for prayer
Holy God:
we trust in your goodness

Holy God, we come to plead for those who suffer
in their pain and weariness.

Silence for prayer

Holy God:
we trust in your goodness

Holy God, we come to plead for the dying
and the bereaved
in their grief and loneliness.

Silence for prayer

Holy God:
we trust in your goodness

Holy God, we come to plead for the coming
of your kingdom
in every place and in every person.

Silence for prayer

Merciful Father,
accept these prayers
for the sake of your Son,
our Saviour Jesus Christ, Amen.

2nd Sunday after Pentecost

YEAR 1

*There's no better feeling than being
restored to the God who loves you
and to whom you belong.*

Father, we lay before you our longing
for many to know the joy and freedom of your service,
and we remember the needs of all
who minister your love and teaching.

Silence for prayer

The Lord will indeed:
give what is good

We lay before you our loathing of corruption
and injustice,
and remember the needs of all peace makers,
negotiators, leaders and advisers.

Silence for prayer

The Lord will indeed:
give what is good

We lay before you our concern for all broken families,
all children being raised in turmoil,
and we remember the needs of all parents.

Silence for prayer

The Lord will indeed:
give what is good

We lay before you our desire to help those
whose lives or bodies are broken through war or abuse
and we remember the needs of all victims.

Silence for prayer

The Lord will indeed:
give what is good

We lay before you our memories
of those we love who have died,
and entrust them to your everlasting care.

Silence for prayer

The Lord will indeed:
give what is good

We lay before you our thankfulness
for the way you come to search for us
whenever we are lost.

Silence for prayer

Merciful Father,
accept these prayers
for the sake of your Son,
our Saviour Jesus Christ, Amen.

YEAR 2

*In Christ we can all belong – he has
broken the barriers down.*

We remember all the clusters of Christians in our area,
and pray that we may truly be one in Christ.
Silence for prayer
Hear, O Lord:
and answer our prayer

We remember all the areas of violence
and hostility in our world,
and pray for peace between nations
and individual people.
Silence for prayer
Hear, O Lord:
and answer our prayer

We remember all families struggling against poverty,
inadequate accommodation or illness,
and pray that you will show us
how best to help them.
Silence for prayer
Hear, O Lord:
and answer our prayer

We remember the vulnerable and the ignored,
the outcasts and the oppressed,
and pray that we may open our hearts
to loving involvement.

Silence for prayer

Hear, O Lord:
and answer our prayer

We remember those who have died
and their loved ones,
and pray that you will comfort all sorrow.

Silence for prayer

Hear, O Lord:
and answer our prayer

We remember with joy your constant loving
and forgiveness,
and pray that we may show our praise
not only with our lips but in our lives.

Silence for prayer

Merciful Father,
accept these prayers
for the sake of your Son,
our Saviour Jesus Christ, Amen.

3rd Sunday after Pentecost

YEAR 1

*New life means revolution,
and it can only happen through God's
freely given power.*

Father, in our Christian ministry to one another
we need more discernment and less defensiveness,
more stillness and less rush.

Silence for prayer

Father, teach us:
to live life your way

Father, in our national and international affairs
we need more listening and less bullying,
more giving and less taking,
more co-operation and less thirst for revenge.

Silence for prayer

Father, teach us:
to live life your way

Father, in our relationships
we need more understanding and less intolerance,
more encouragement and less condemnation.

Silence for prayer

Father, teach us:
to live life your way

Father, in our pain we need your comfort,
in our brokenness your forgiveness,
in our anguish the assurance of your love.

Silence for prayer

Father, teach us:
to live life your way

Father, at the hour of our death
we need your presence and your mercy.

Silence for prayer

Father, teach us:
to live life your way

Father, in you our every need is met and satisfied,
and we thank you for the personal love
you have for each one of us.

Silence for prayer

Merciful Father,
accept these prayers
for the sake of your Son,
our Saviour Jesus Christ, Amen.

YEAR 2

*The kingdom of God is righteousness
taking root in individuals and so
affecting the whole of society for good.*

We pray that your church will have courage
to speak up for what is right and loving;
we pray for those who are persecuted
or imprisoned because of their faith.
Silence for prayer
Father, fill us up:
with goodness and with love

We pray for integrity and wisdom
in all who advise and lead in our world;
we pray for the areas where law and order
have broken down.
Silence for prayer
Father, fill us up:
with goodness and with love

We pray that our homes may be places of welcome,
comfort and friendship;
we pray for all who will walk in and out
of our homes this week.
Silence for prayer
Father, fill us up:
with goodness and with love

We pray for all who are victims of greed,
cruelty and revenge;
we pray for those who hate,
and all who are finding it difficult to forgive.

Silence for prayer

Father, fill us up:
with goodness and with love

We pray for those who have come to the end
of their earthly life,
and those who mourn.

Silence for prayer

Father, fill us up:
with goodness and with love

We praise and bless you for every scrap
of tenderness,
every spark of joy,
and every glimpse of your glory.

Silence for prayer

Merciful Father,
accept these prayers
for the sake of your Son,
our Saviour Jesus Christ, Amen.

4th Sunday
after Pentecost

YEAR 1

*True freedom neither means doing
what you like, nor being trapped by
someone else's sin.*

Father, we pray for all church leaders,
and all who minister to others through their teaching
of the faith.
Keep us available to encourage them
and help them wherever we can.

Silence for prayer

My soul is thirsty for God:
thirsty for the living God

We pray for those who influence the thinking
and general behaviour of people all over the world;
for clear guidance in what is right and true.

Silence for prayer

My soul is thirsty for God:
thirsty for the living God

We pray for all those entrusted with the responsibility
of bringing up children;
and for all those who are finding adolescence difficult.

Silence for prayer

My soul is thirsty for God:
thirsty for the living God

We pray for all whose lives are restricted
through illness, disability or frailty;
we pray for all imprisoned by addiction.

Silence for prayer

My soul is thirsty for God:
thirsty for the living God

We pray for those who have died
and for those who are finding life bleak
without them.

Silence for prayer

My soul is thirsty for God:
thirsty for the living God

We pray with thankfulness for every reconciliation,
every flame of love and tenderness,
every word of forgiveness
and every act of loving care.

Silence for prayer

Merciful Father,
accept these prayers
for the sake of your Son,
our Saviour Jesus Christ, Amen.

YEAR 2

*God tells each of us our own story
and loves us into his kingdom.*

Father, the church has its areas of weakness and pain;
we long to be truly and faithfully
the body of Christ.

Silence for prayer

Father, we thank you:
for hearing our needs

Father, the nations bicker and fight;
we long for a world where love
and peace prevail.

Silence for prayer

Father, we thank you:
for hearing our needs

Father, our homes and families have tensions
and misunderstandings;
we long for your wise parenting in every home.

Silence for prayer

Father, we thank you:
for hearing our needs

Father, many are sad, stressed, in pain or in need;
we long for your healing presence
to comfort and renew.

Silence for prayer

Father, we thank you:
for hearing our needs

Father, some die destitute and unnoticed;
some die violently,
and many grieve for their loved ones;
we long for your reassuring love and hope.

Silence for prayer

Father, we thank you:
for hearing our needs

Father, our lives are so rich with blessings;
we long to show our thanks in our lives.

Silence for prayer

Merciful Father,
accept these prayers
for the sake of your Son,
our Saviour Jesus Christ, Amen.

5th Sunday after Pentecost

YEAR 1

*If we really understood God's law
it would drive us weeping to his feet.*

We ask you to fill us with delight at doing
your will, and at bringing others to know you.
Refresh those whose faith is dry and stiff.

Silence for prayer

Father, take us over:
both inside and out

We ask for integrity in our own parish,
in local and world decisions.

Silence for prayer

Father, take us over:
both inside and out

We ask for clear guidance in medical ethics,
and the courage to stand up for your values.

Silence for prayer

Father, take us over:
both inside and out

We ask that you will welcome into your kingdom
all those who have recently died,
and we ask you to prepare us on earth
to live with you in heaven.

Silence for prayer

Father, take us over:
both inside and out

We ask for the grace to live joyfully
as we travel with you through our lives,
and remember now all that you have done for us.

Silence for prayer

Merciful Father,
accept these prayers
for the sake of your Son,
our Saviour Jesus Christ, Amen.

YEAR 2

God's saving news of love is not for a few,
but for every person in every nation.

Father, set your church on fire with your love
for everyone, without exception.
Silence for prayer
Take us, Lord:
and use us wherever you need us

Father, let the greed and selfishness
which tear our world apart,
be overcome with generosity of spirit
and concern for one another's good.
Silence for prayer
Take us, Lord:
and use us wherever you need us

Father, let every home become a place of comfort;
safe, happy and welcoming.
Silence for prayer
Take us, Lord:
and use us wherever you need us

Father, let those who are distressed
and diseased find healing, refreshment
and meaning for their lives.
Silence for prayer
Take us, Lord:
and use us wherever you need us

Father, let those who have died
spend their eternity with you,
at peace and in joy for ever;
and may their loved ones be comforted
in their sorrow.

Silence for prayer

Take us, Lord:
and use us wherever you need us

Father, may we shine as lights
as you draw all people
to fulfilment in you.

Silence for prayer

Merciful Father,
accept these prayers
for the sake of your Son,
our Saviour Jesus Christ, Amen.

6th Sunday after Pentecost

YEAR 1

*In Jesus we are not just patched up
but made new.*

In the chapels, churches and cathedrals,
and in every gathering of Christians,
God all-knowing, God all-loving:
come, make us new
Silence for prayer

Where faith is frayed, where prayer is casual,
where God is patronised
and the harvest is ignored,
God all-knowing, God all-loving:
come, make us new
Silence for prayer

In the homes, shops, schools
and meeting places of our town,
in the conversations we have this week,
God all-knowing, God all-loving:
come, make us new
Silence for prayer

Where people are sad or burdened with guilt,
where illness and frailty are hard to bear cheerfully,
God all-knowing, God all-loving:
come, make us new

Silence for prayer

As those we have known and love
journey from this life into eternity,
and we call to mind that heaven is our home,
God all-knowing, God all-loving:
come, make us new

Silence for prayer

In our moments and days,
our sorrows and our joys,
God all-knowing, God all-loving:
come, make us new

Silence for prayer

Merciful Father,
accept these prayers
for the sake of your Son,
our Saviour Jesus Christ, Amen.

YEAR 2

*In Jesus we are not just patched up
but made new.*

Thank you, Father, for the patient love
you show in teaching and guiding us,
challenging and coaxing us.
We ask you to bless each person
on their journey of faith.
Silence for prayer
Your ways are holy, Lord:
and your ways are best

Thank you, Father, for every peace initiative,
each act of goodness, each victory over evil.
Bless and guide the nations of our world.
Silence for prayer
Your ways are holy, Lord:
and your ways are best

Thank you, Father, for the friendships we cherish,
for the members of our families,
and for our neighbours.
Bless each home with your presence.
Silence for prayer
Your ways are holy, Lord:
and your ways are best

Thank you, Father, for all who care for the sick,
the very young and the very old.
Bless all who suffer with the comfort of your love.
Silence for prayer

Your ways are holy, Lord:
and your ways are best

Thank you, Father, for the example of lives well lived
and death honestly and bravely faced.
Welcome into your kingdom all who have died in faith,
and those whose faith is known only to you.
Silence for prayer

Your ways are holy, Lord:
and your ways are best

Thank you, Father, for all the abundance
of life you provide for us.
Silence for prayer

Merciful Father,
accept these prayers
for the sake of your Son,
our Saviour Jesus Christ, Amen.

7th Sunday
after Pentecost

YEAR 1

*Since we are made in God's likeness,
the only real and fulfilling way to live
is in a loving, Godlike way.*

Father, we call to mind the world church;
we acknowledge our divisions and mistakes
and thank you for transforming them
even as we pray.
Silence for prayer
Teach us, Lord:
to walk in your light

Father, we call to mind the wounds of our world
born of collective greed and terrible blunders
throughout history;
and we praise you as you work to bring wholeness.
Silence for prayer
Teach us, Lord:
to walk in your light

Father, we call to mind the nurturing of children
and the responsibility of parenthood and community;
we need your guidance and grace,
your protection and courage.

Silence for prayer

Teach us, Lord:
to walk in your light

Father, we call to mind those trapped in addictions,
imprisoned by guilt,
and drained through grief;
on their behalf, we plead for rescue.

Silence for prayer

Teach us, Lord:
to walk in your light

Father, we call to mind those who have died,
and those who are dying now,
unnoticed and unloved.

Silence for prayer

Teach us, Lord:
to walk in your light

Father, we call to mind the way you have
dealt with us so lovingly in the past,
and we commit our future into your keeping.

Silence for prayer

Merciful Father,
accept these prayers
for the sake of your Son,
our Saviour Jesus Christ, Amen.

YEAR 2

We are to love others in the way God
loves us – completely.

Father, we pray that all Christians may grow
more loving, more active and more faithful,
starting now.
Silence for prayer
God is greater than our hearts:
and he knows everything

Father, we pray for all world leaders
and those who advise them,
that they may make good decisions
and act wisely.
Silence for prayer
God is greater than our hearts:
and he knows everything

Father, we pray for single parent families,
families under stress and all who are
separated from loved ones.
Silence for prayer
God is greater than our hearts:
and he knows everything

Father, we pray for the mentally ill,
the physically damaged,
for the lonely and the fearful.

Silence for prayer

God is greater than our hearts:
and he knows everything

Father, we pray for those who have come
to the end of their earthly life,
and for those who miss them,
or never had the opportunity
to put things right with them.

Silence for prayer

God is greater than our hearts:
and he knows everything

Father, we bring to you our secret hopes
and longings and our gratitude.

Silence for prayer

Merciful Father,
accept these prayers
for the sake of your Son,
our Saviour Jesus Christ, Amen.

8th Sunday after Pentecost

YEAR 1

What we are determines how we fruit.

In your presence we bring to mind all Christians;
those recently baptised or recently returned to the faith,
all church leaders and those whose faith is hesitant.

Silence for prayer

From eternity to eternity:
you are God

In your presence we call to mind the areas
of conflict, righteous anger and hardened attitudes,
and we pray for your lasting peace.

Silence for prayer

From eternity to eternity:
you are God

In your presence we bring to mind those
who have influenced our faith development,
those we love, and those who love us.

Silence for prayer

From eternity to eternity:
you are God

In your presence we call to mind those
who are enchained by guilt,
or bad and frightening memories
which need to be released.

Silence for prayer

From eternity to eternity:
you are God

In your presence we call to mind those
who have died and moved from time into eternity;
their families and all who miss them.

Silence for prayer

From eternity to eternity:
you are God

In your presence we bring to mind the beauty,
love and peace which surround us
and bubble up even inside pain and grief.

Silence for prayer

Merciful Father,
accept these prayers
for the sake of your Son,
our Saviour Jesus Christ, Amen.

YEAR 2

What we are determines how we fruit.

Father, you know our motives as well as our actions;
bless our decision-making,
so that we do not make wrong choices in our lives.
Silence for prayer
Teach us your ways:
and help us to live them

Father, you know the strengths
and weaknesses of our church;
we do not want to hide anything away,
but long for your advice and guidance.
Silence for prayer
Teach us your ways:
and help us to live them

Father, you know us, and those we live and work with;
you understand the real reasons
for our quarrels and upsets;
we long for you to work your healing
in those hidden areas.
Silence for prayer
Teach us your ways:
and help us to live them

Father, you know the individual history
behind each person's revenge
and each country's difficulties;
we long for peace and tranquillity in our world.

Silence for prayer

Teach us your ways:
and help us to live them

Father, you watch with the sick and the dying;
you feel their pain and know their fear;
we long for them to know your loving
presence with them.

Silence for prayer

Teach us your ways:
and help us to live them

Father, your creation is indeed very good,
and we praise and thank you for all you provide.

Silence for prayer

Merciful Father,
accept these prayers
for the sake of your Son,
our Saviour Jesus Christ, Amen.

9th Sunday after Pentecost

YEAR 1

*God's protection against evil will
enable us to get on with his work.*

Father, we pray for the building up of your church;
for each individual member as we struggle
with doubts, fears and weariness,
with scorn or persecution.

Silence for prayer

From eternity to eternity:
you are our God

Father, we pray for the building of peace
between nations,
the building of honour and respect between people,
as we work through deep hurts from the past.

Silence for prayer

From eternity to eternity:
you are our God

Father, we pray for the building up of communities
in areas where people feel lost and like strangers;
for a sense of trust and mutual support.

Silence for prayer

From eternity to eternity:
you are our God

Father, we pray for those recovering
from surgery and illness;
for those who lack energy and vitality;
for those who cannot face the future.

Silence for prayer

From eternity to eternity:
you are our God

Father, we pray for those who have finished
their earthly life and now enter eternity;
and we pray for those who badly miss
their physical presence.

Silence for prayer

From eternity to eternity:
you are our God

Father, we pray that we may increasingly
notice your glory,
delight in your care of us
and rest in your peace.

Silence for prayer

Merciful Father,
accept these prayers
for the sake of your Son,
our Saviour Jesus Christ, Amen.

YEAR 2

God's protection against evil will
enable us to get on with his work.

Father, we commend to your love
all church leaders and those in their care;
all who need encouragement and reassurance.
Silence for prayer
May the favour of the Lord:
rest upon us

Father, we commend to your mercy
all the areas of violence in our world;
the hopes and disillusions,
the potential good and evil.
Silence for prayer
May the favour of the Lord:
rest upon us

Father, we commend to your tenderness
our relatives and friends,
both those who bring joy
and those who cause us great concern.
Silence for prayer
May the favour of the Lord:
rest upon us

Father, we commend to your loving care
all whose lives are caged by guilt or terror;
all who are coming to terms with a disability;
all who suffer through another's cruelty.

Silence for prayer

May the favour of the Lord:
rest upon us

Father, we commend to your welcoming arms
those who have arrived at the point of death,
especially the unnoticed and uncared for.

Silence for prayer

May the favour of the Lord:
rest upon us

Father, we commend to you our thanks and praise
for all that is good and beautiful,
responsive and true.

Silence for prayer

Merciful Father,
**accept these prayers
for the sake of your Son,
our Saviour Jesus Christ, Amen.**

10th Sunday after Pentecost

YEAR 1

*God's wisdom turns our priorities
upside down.*

Father, let your light stream into every Christian life
to show up anything that needs cutting out, healing,
renewing, softening or purifying.
Silence for prayer
Help us to think with your mind:
and love with your heart

Father, let your wisdom take control
in all decisions and advice,
all legislation and negotiation.
Silence for prayer
Help us to think with your mind:
and love with your heart

Father, let the warmth of your love
be present in every home
and in every relationship,
in our celebrations and our struggles.
Silence for prayer
Help us to think with your mind:
and love with your heart

Father, let the power of your healing bring to wholeness
those who are disturbed and agitated,
suffering in body or mind or spirit.

Silence for prayer

Help us to think with your mind:
and love with your heart

Father, let your loving mercy bring the dead and dying
safely home to heaven,
and give comfort to those who mourn.

Silence for prayer

Help us to think with your mind:
and love with your heart

Father, let your joy fill our lives
as we delight in living according to your ways.

Silence for prayer

Merciful Father,
accept these prayers
for the sake of your Son,
our Saviour Jesus Christ, Amen.

YEAR 2

God's wisdom turns our priorities
upside down.

Father, we call to mind the church and its leaders,
all who minister in word and sacrament;
a church divided, with problems, hopes
and responsibilities.
Silence for prayer
My God and my all:
my God and my all

Father, we call to mind the barren areas of our world
and the areas of abundance and wealth;
the crowded cities and isolated communities,
the squalid, the fashionable, the oppressed
and the endangered.
Silence for prayer
My God and my all:
my God and my all

Father, we call to mind our parents
and all whom we love and care for;
all who cause us concern, all who make us laugh
and all whose lives touch our own.
Silence for prayer
My God and my all:
my God and my all

Father, we call to mind the malnourished
and the starving;
those living in inadequate housing
and those with nowhere to live.

Silence for prayer

My God and my all:
my God and my all

Father, we call to mind the dying,
and those who have finished their earthly life;
those who die alone and those who grieve alone.

Silence for prayer

My God and my all:
my God and my all

Father, we call to mind all that is good
and lovely in our lives; all that builds us up,
eases our loads and strengthens our faith.

Silence for prayer

Merciful Father,
accept these prayers
for the sake of your Son,
our Saviour Jesus Christ, Amen.

11th Sunday after Pentecost

YEAR 1

*It's not God's will that we burn
ourselves out, but that we support and
encourage one another as we serve
those in need.*

For all church leaders, bishops, priests and deacons;
for all who are overworked and stressed;
for all who feel they are doing an impossible job;
let us pray.

Silence for prayer

Our help is in the name of the Lord:
who has made heaven and earth

For all world leaders and their advisers;
for judges, and all who work to uphold law and order;
for leaders of oppressive and corrupt regimes;
let us pray.

Silence for prayer

Our help is in the name of the Lord:
who has made heaven and earth

For families coping with difficulties;
for children suffering abuse or neglect;
for those we love, and those we dislike;
let us pray.

Silence for prayer

Our help is in the name of the Lord:
who has made heaven and earth

For all who are dependent on others for everyday care;
for the crippled in body and the confused of mind;
for the victims of violence, carelessness and hatred;
let us pray.

Silence for prayer

Our help is in the name of the Lord:
who has made heaven and earth

For those who are dying, even as we pray;
for those facing death with terror;
for all who have recently gone through
the journey of death;
let us pray.

Silence for prayer

Our help is in the name of the Lord:
who has made heaven and earth

For all that lightens our lives with laughter,
for all that blesses our lives with peace,
let us give God thanks and praise.

Silence for prayer

Merciful Father,
accept these prayers
for the sake of your Son,
our Saviour Jesus Christ, Amen.

YEAR 2

*It's not God's will that we burden one
another, but that we give one another
encouragement and support.*

Father, we bring to you the disunity in the church
which so many are dedicated to heal;
we bring the efforts for reconciliation,
and our longing to live out your will in our lives.
Silence for prayer

With our God:
nothing is impossible

Father, we bring to you the fragile nature
of our humanity,
our efforts and mistakes in caring for this world;
our leaders, our talks and conferences, our decisions.
Silence for prayer

With our God:
nothing is impossible

Father, we bring to you the homes and families
we represent;
the homes in our neighbourhood;
the children attending our local schools.
Silence for prayer

With our God:
nothing is impossible

Father, we bring to you all who carry burdens
and have no one to share the weight;
we bring the ill, the weary, the frightened
and the homeless.

Silence for prayer

With our God:
nothing is impossible

Father, we bring to you those who have died
and those who grieve at their going.
We bring those who die unnoticed and in despair.

Silence for prayer

With our God:
nothing is impossible

Father, we bring to you our thanks
for your unchanging love
and your affection for us;
we bring our desire to love you more and more.

Silence for prayer

Merciful Father,
accept these prayers
for the sake of your Son,
our Saviour Jesus Christ, Amen.

12th Sunday after Pentecost

YEAR 1

It is both our privilege and our responsibility to spread the good news wherever we are put.

We pray for all missionaries and evangelists,
particularly those who are ridiculed or persecuted
for their faith;
we pray for all who hear your word,
that they may receive it with joy.

Silence for prayer

In your strength, Lord:
make us strong

We pray for those in local, national
and international government;
for integrity and sensitivity in all debates;
for right judgements, good counsel and fair laws.

Silence for prayer

In your strength, Lord:
make us strong

We pray for our homes and all who live or visit there;
that each room may be blessed with your love
to nurture forgiveness, mutual respect and compassion.

Silence for prayer

In your strength, Lord:
make us strong

We pray for those whose bodies are weak,
whose minds are blurred, whose spirits are listless;
we pray for comfort, healing, refreshment and peace.

Silence for prayer

In your strength, Lord:
make us strong

We pray for those whose life on earth has ended,
that you will welcome them with mercy
into your kingdom;
we pray for those who have died violently
and for those who struggle to forgive.

Silence for prayer

In your strength, Lord:
make us strong

We pray for the truth of your astounding love
to reach deeper into our understanding as we praise
and bless your name in our lives.

Silence for prayer

Merciful Father,
accept these prayers
for the sake of your Son,
our Saviour Jesus Christ, Amen.

YEAR 2

*It is both our privilege and our
responsibility to spread the good news
wherever we are put.*

Whenever we face obstacles in living God's way;
whenever the church is called to stand for what is right;
whenever we find God using us for his glory,
Father, we need your help.

Silence for prayer

At all times and in all places:
we praise the God of love

When past wounds keep nations from working together;
wherever power threatens to corrupt;
when injustices need righting,
Father, we need your help.

Silence for prayer

At all times and in all places:
we praise the God of love

When the children squabble and the grown-ups nag;
when anyone feels left out or unacceptable,
Father, we need your help.

Silence for prayer

At all times and in all places:
we praise the God of love

When pain takes over, and normality is only a dream;
when carers grow weary and tempers fray;
when sleep won't come and waking is unwelcome,
Father, we need your help.

Silence for prayer

At all times and in all places:
we praise the God of love

When the stars or sunlight touch our hearts
with wonder;
when we catch a glimpse of your tenderness or power,
Father, we give you our thanks.

Silence for prayer

Merciful Father,
accept these prayers
for the sake of your Son,
our Saviour Jesus Christ, Amen.

13th Sunday after Pentecost

YEAR 1

Being a Christian doesn't take all the suffering away, but transforms our way of dealing with it.

We call to mind our brothers and sisters in Christ
who are imprisoned or suffering persecution
simply for believing what we believe.
Silence for prayer
Trust in the Lord:
for with the Lord there is mercy

We call to mind those whose lives
are caught up in war, political unrest,
family feuds or nationalistic grievances.
Silence for prayer
Trust in the Lord:
for with the Lord there is mercy

We call to mind refugees and all who do not know
whether their loved ones are safe or not;
all whose homes are places of violence
and all whose homes are havens of love.
Silence for prayer
Trust in the Lord:
for with the Lord there is mercy

We call to mind those imprisoned by guilt,
addiction or bitterness;
and all those who undergo suffering bravely
and bring joy to those who care for them.

Silence for prayer

Trust in the Lord:
for with the Lord there is mercy

We call to mind those who have recently died
and those who miss them;
those who are nearing death,
and those who support them.

Silence for prayer

Trust in the Lord:
for with the Lord there is mercy

We call to mind the times when God
has carried us through difficulties,
and thank him for his faithful love.

Silence for prayer

Merciful Father,
accept these prayers
for the sake of your Son,
our Saviour Jesus Christ, Amen.

YEAR 2

*Being a Christian doesn't take all the
suffering away, but transforms our
way of dealing with it.*

Father, we remember those whose faith is
fresh and fragile, those who labour
faithfully in your service through difficult times;
all who minister by word and sacrament
throughout the church.
Silence for prayer
Come, Lord:
comfort your people

Father, we remember the needs of the world
and the unbalanced spread of wealth;
we remember the leaders and advisers,
the peace makers and the law makers.
Silence for prayer
Come, Lord:
comfort your people

Father, we remember our own relatives and friends,
our neighbours and those we meet week by week;
we remember the laughter and tears we have shared,
the hopes, dreams and fears.
Silence for prayer
Come, Lord:
comfort your people

Father, we remember the weary and heavily burdened,
the anxious, and those who have lost their way;
all whose lives are filled with suffering;
all who do not yet know Jesus.

Silence for prayer

Come, Lord:
comfort your people

Father, we remember those
who have come to the end of their earthly life
and those who have nursed and cared for them
and will miss their physical presence.

Silence for prayer

Come, Lord:
comfort your people

Father, we remember your kindness and mercy
to us at every stage of our journey,
and offer you our thanks and praise.

Silence for prayer

Merciful Father,
accept these prayers
for the sake of your Son,
our Saviour Jesus Christ, Amen.

14th Sunday
after Pentecost

YEAR 1

Whatever our age or marital status,
we are all children in God's family,
brothers and sisters bound together by love.

Father, we bring to you our longing for unity,
our desire for a closer walk with you
and our concern for all our Christian
brothers and sisters.

Silence for prayer

God is full of compassion:
full of compassion and love

Father, we bring to you our longing
for a world of peace and integrity;
a world of mutual respect
and international understanding.

Silence for prayer

God is full of compassion:
full of compassion and love

Father, we bring to you our love and concern
for our families, friends and neighbours;
particularly those facing change or feeling isolated.

Silence for prayer

God is full of compassion:
full of compassion and love

Father, we bring to you our desire for healing
and wholeness in those who are distressed,
uncomfortable or in great pain;
we bring our willingness to help
wherever you want to use us.

Silence for prayer

God is full of compassion:
full of compassion and love

Father, we bring to you our loved ones who have died,
and those who are dying with no one near them.

Silence for prayer

God is full of compassion:
full of compassion and love

Father, we bring to you our thanks for life
and all its blessings;
for the experiences we learn from and grow through.

Silence for prayer

Merciful Father,
**accept these prayers
for the sake of your Son,
our Saviour Jesus Christ, Amen.**

YEAR 2

Whatever our age or marital status,
we are all children in God's family,
brothers and sisters bound together by love.

Father, we thank you for welcoming us
into your family;
for treating us as special and forgiving us.
We pray for all our Christian brothers and sisters
worshipping today all over the world.
Silence for prayer

Thank you, Father:
for loving us so much

Father, we think of our parents
and all who have helped and looked after us
through our life;
we pray that you will make your home
in our homes.
Silence for prayer

Thank you, Father:
for loving us so much

Father, we pray for those damaged
through bad relationships;
those who are lonely, rejected or broken-hearted;
we pray for the newly born and their parents.
Silence for prayer

Thank you, Father:
for loving us so much

Father, we remember those who have reached death
and ask that you will welcome them
into your kingdom.

Silence for prayer

Thank you, Father:
for loving us so much

Father, we thank you for the opportunities
to practise forgiveness;
for the different times that have enabled us to grow;
for the light-hearted times that have made us happy.

Silence for prayer

Merciful Father,
accept these prayers
for the sake of your Son,
our Saviour Jesus Christ, Amen.

15th Sunday after Pentecost

YEAR 1

*God is the One who has power over
our lives and everything we do.*

We pray for the churches which are thriving
and those which have lost a sense
of your direction;
we pray for a reckless giving of ourselves to God.
Silence for prayer
Lord, our God:
let your will be done in us

We pray for those in positions of power and authority;
we pray against all corruption and personal ego-trips;
we pray for justice, mutual respect, peace and humility.
Silence for prayer
Lord, our God:
let your will be done in us

We pray for those who make us feel happy
and comfortable,
and for those we find it hard to get on with;
we pray for all who take care of children.
Silence for prayer
Lord, our God:
let your will be done in us

We pray for those whose minds or bodies
are trapped in illness,
those who lack freedom of movement;
we pray for all involved in medical research.

Silence for prayer

Lord, our God:
let your will be done in us

We pray for the dead and the dying,
for those dying without care or comfort;
for all victims of violence.

Silence for prayer

Lord, our God:
let your will be done in us

We pray for a deeper understanding of God
as we remember with thankfulness
the constant faithfulness and love which surround us.

Silence for prayer

Merciful Father,
accept these prayers
for the sake of your Son,
our Saviour Jesus Christ, Amen.

YEAR 2

*God is the One who has power over
our lives and everything we do.*

We call to mind all church leaders
and the problems they face;
all ministers, evangelists, teachers and healers;
all who come thirsting and searching for God.

Silence for prayer

We are your people, O Lord:
and you are our God

We call to mind the nations and their leaders;
the temptations that accompany power
and the people's needs and hardships.

Silence for prayer

We are your people, O Lord:
and you are our God

We call to mind each home in this area;
the squabbles and tears, the laughter and affection.

Silence for prayer

We are your people, O Lord:
and you are our God

We call to mind those in hospital and at home
who are in pain;
those who are frightened by their illness;
and all who care for them.

Silence for prayer

We are your people, O Lord:
and you are our God

We call to mind those who have recently died
and can meet you face to face;
those for whom death is terrifying
and all who are unprepared.

Silence for prayer

We are your people, O Lord:
and you are our God

We call to mind the glimpses of glory you show us;
the times when we have known your presence
close to us;
the times of unexpected joy.

Silence for prayer

Merciful Father,
accept these prayers
for the sake of your Son,
our Saviour Jesus Christ, Amen.

16th Sunday after Pentecost

YEAR 1

*Treat others as you want them to
treat you.*

Where the church is weakened by doubt or apathy,
by confused priorities, or lack of self discipline,
we commend it to the Father's love.

Silence for prayer

Father, we ask not for what we want:
but for what you know we need

Where the world is morally off course,
bogged down in ancient feuds,
and overwhelmed with disaster,
we commend it to the Father's love.

Silence for prayer

Father, we ask not for what we want:
but for what you know we need

Where homes are harassed and over-busy,
where children are frightened
or adults are coping in difficult circumstances,
we commend them to the Father's love.

Silence for prayer

Father, we ask not for what we want:
but for what you know we need

Where patients wait for and recover from operations,
where the helpless are learning dependence
and today's new babies are struggling into the world,
we commend them to the Father's love.

Silence for prayer

Father, we ask not for what we want:
but for what you know we need

Where the dying are entering eternity,
and the suffering bodies are at last
relieved of pain,
we commend them to the Father's love.

Silence for prayer

Father, we ask not for what we want:
but for what you know we need

Where experience has taught us more of God's love;
where friends and neighbours have enriched our lives,
we offer, Father, our thanks and praise.

Silence for prayer

Merciful Father,
accept these prayers
for the sake of your Son,
our Saviour Jesus Christ, Amen.

YEAR 2

Treat others as you want them to treat you.

Father, we remember our brothers and sisters in Christ
as they worship in large and small groups
all over the world.

Silence for prayer

O give thanks to the Lord:
for he is good

Father, we think of the world's peacemakers
and all who spend their lives
working constructively for good;
all who uphold Christian values and stand firm
for what is right.

Silence for prayer

O give thanks to the Lord:
for he is good

Father, we remember all who are
bringing their children up carefully and lovingly;
all who care for elderly neighbours and relatives;
all who work to build community where they live.

Silence for prayer

O give thanks to the Lord:
for he is good

Father, we think of the sick and those caring for them;
we think of those who rarely get a break,
but need one;
those who are offering their suffering for you to use.

Silence for prayer

O give thanks to the Lord:
for he is good

Father, we remember those who are dying
and those who have crossed from time into eternity;
we think of the example of their lives
and we remember those who love them.

Silence for prayer

O give thanks to the Lord:
for he is good

Father, we think of the beauty of all you have made
and the daily miracles of life and love.

Silence for prayer

Merciful Father,
**accept these prayers
for the sake of your Son,
our Saviour Jesus Christ, Amen.**

17th Sunday after Pentecost

YEAR 1

Work for God's glory, not your own.

Father, we entrust to you the small
and the complex problems
facing your church throughout the world;
we think of all those in lay and ordained ministry
and of each person worshipping somewhere today.

Silence for prayer

You are my refuge:
God in whom I trust

Father, we entrust to you the local issues
where feelings run high;
the national and international matters of concern
and our longing for your kingdom to come on earth.

Silence for prayer

You are my refuge:
God in whom I trust

Father, we entrust to you our loved ones;
those who are constantly on our minds;
those who frighten us;
and all who need us to listen to them better.

Silence for prayer

You are my refuge:
God in whom I trust

Father, we entrust to you all who feel lost
or disillusioned;
those whose lives are plagued by resentment
or guilt;
all who suffer and need comforting.

Silence for prayer

You are my refuge:
God in whom I trust

Father, we entrust to you those who have died
and those who will die today;
all who mourn and all who minister
to their needs.

Silence for prayer

You are my refuge:
God in whom I trust

Father, we entrust to you ourselves
and the rest of our lives;
all our decisions,
hopes, sorrows and joys.

Silence for prayer

Merciful Father,
**accept these prayers
for the sake of your Son,
our Saviour Jesus Christ, Amen.**

YEAR 2

Work for God's glory, not your own.

Father, we ask you to strengthen
and purify your people;
teach us to be better listeners to each other
and to you.
Speak to our inmost being and show us your will.

Silence for prayer

When we call:
we know you answer us

Father, we ask you to unravel the tangled problems
of our world;
help us to follow you, step by step,
towards harmony and peace.

Silence for prayer

When we call:
we know you answer us

Father, we ask you to live in our homes
and in all hostels and orphanages.
Remind us to value the time we spend with our friends
and listen to one another with full attention.

Silence for prayer

When we call:
we know you answer us

Father, we ask that the sick and injured
will be aware of your comforting presence;
that the very old and the very young
may know they are safe and loved.

Silence for prayer

When we call:
we know you answer us

Father, we ask you to welcome into your kingdom
those who have recently travelled through death
from lifetimes all over the world.

Silence for prayer

When we call:
we know you answer us

Father, we ask you to sharpen our awareness
of all that is beautiful, hopeful,
precious and eternal.

Silence for prayer

Merciful Father,
accept these prayers
for the sake of your Son,
our Saviour Jesus Christ, Amen.

18th Sunday
after Pentecost

YEAR 1

Live every day of your life to the full.

Father, we give you thanks for your constant care
of the church in all its strengths and weaknesses;
for your sensitive guiding, pruning,
anointing and enabling.

Silence for prayer

The Lord is my strength:
the Lord is my strength and my song

Father, we give you thanks for your love
which binds up the world's woundings,
protects and defends us against evil,
and works unceasingly for what is right and just.

Silence for prayer

The Lord is my strength:
the Lord is my strength and my song

Father, we give you thanks for your presence
in our homes through the nights and mornings,
afternoons and evenings,
each day, each week, each year.

Silence for prayer

The Lord is my strength:
the Lord is my strength and my song

Father, we give you thanks for your comfort
which refreshes and soothes, supports and sustains
all who are sick in body, mind or spirit.

Silence for prayer

The Lord is my strength:
the Lord is my strength and my song

Father, we give you thanks for life
which is not taken away at death
but brought into fullness and everlasting peace.

Silence for prayer

Merciful Father,
accept these prayers
for the sake of your Son,
our Saviour Jesus Christ, Amen.

YEAR 2

Live every day of your life to the full.

Father, in all our preparation for worship,
in our committees and various groups and meetings,
be among us to work in us,
with us and through us.
Silence for prayer
Holy God:
take charge

Father, in all our political debates and congresses,
in the hidden agendas and the gaps between words,
work your will and prepare our hearts
to work with you.
Silence for prayer
Holy God:
take charge

Father, in all our times of shared laughter
and shared tears,
in our efforts to reconcile,
and our failures to please,
touch our lives with your compassion and affection.
Silence for prayer
Holy God:
take charge

Father, in all the pain and suffering
of our brothers and sisters,
in the times which come close to despair,
lift us on your shoulders and carry us to safety.

Silence for prayer

Holy God:
take charge

Father, as we release into your everlasting protection
those who have recently died,
renew and deepen our understanding
of what it means to have the gift of eternal life.

Silence for prayer

Holy God:
take charge

Father, in all that we say and do during this week
may we know the freshness of your love
and the security of your hold on us.

Silence for prayer

Merciful Father,
accept these prayers
for the sake of your Son,
our Saviour Jesus Christ, Amen.

19th Sunday
after Pentecost

YEAR 1

Commit your ways to God;
he promises to look after your needs
and he will not let you down.

Father, increase our faith;
help us to grow closer and closer to you
as we live and pray and worship.
Silence for prayer
Lord, we believe:
help our unbelief

Father, open the hearts and minds of all leaders
so that your will is done
and your kingdom spreads throughout
the whole world.
Silence for prayer
Lord, we believe:
help our unbelief

Father, speak your love through our voices
and our actions, in our homes, our places of work,
and wherever we go.
Silence for prayer
Lord, we believe:
help our unbelief

Father, let your comforting and healing presence
touch those who suffer
and those who are frightened,
to fill them with peace.

Silence for prayer

Lord, we believe:
help our unbelief

Father, gather to yourself the souls of those
who have finished their earthly life,
and comfort those who mourn their going.

Silence for prayer

Lord, we believe:
help our unbelief

Father, we offer you our thanks and praise
for all the signs of your glory we experience
and cherish.

Silence for prayer

Merciful Father,
accept these prayers
for the sake of your Son,
our Saviour Jesus Christ, Amen.

YEAR 2

Commit your ways to God;
he promises to look after your needs
and he will not let you down.

Through the adventures of Christian witness
and the dangers, insults, mocking and anger
we may meet,
keep us, and all your church, loyal and strong.
Silence for prayer
Come with us, Lord:
and we will go with you

Through the local, national and international tensions,
through rows in the community
and distortions of the truth,
keep us and all people honest,
just and compassionate.
Silence for prayer
Come with us, Lord:
and we will go with you

Through the interrupted nights,
the quarrels and celebrations,
the unspoken needs and wounds,
keep us and our children safe and loving.
Silence for prayer
Come with us, Lord:
and we will go with you

Through the dark hours of pain,
the struggle with guilt and the damage of hatred,
keep us trustful and open.

Silence for prayer

Come with us, Lord:
and we will go with you

Through the last journey of death
and the ache of separation,
keep us both in and out of time,
held firmly by your love.

Silence for prayer

Come with us, Lord:
and we will go with you

Through the sunlight and shadows of each day,
through storms and stillness,
keep us thankful and rejoicing.

Silence for prayer

Merciful Father,
accept these prayers
for the sake of your Son,
our Saviour Jesus Christ, Amen.

20th Sunday after Pentecost

YEAR 1

If we endure, we shall reign with him.

God of holiness, cleanse the church
from all that is selfish, complacent and worldly.
Silence for prayer
His love goes on:
his love goes on and on

God of wisdom and honour, give our leaders integrity,
and our world the openness to listen,
and the courage to forgive.
Silence for prayer
His love goes on:
his love goes on and on

God of tenderness and understanding,
may our children be brought up
in the knowledge of your love
and every member of every family be valued.
Silence for prayer
His love goes on:
his love goes on and on

God of healing and wholeness,
give to those who are in any pain or suffering
all that they need,
both physically and spiritually.

Silence for prayer

His love goes on:
his love goes on and on

God of eternity, as you welcome into your kingdom
those who have endured to the end,
we thank you for the example of their lives.

Silence for prayer

His love goes on:
his love goes on and on

God of joy and serenity, we thank you
for your constant help and loving presence,
and offer you our lives, however things turn out.

Silence for prayer

Merciful Father,
accept these prayers
for the sake of your Son,
our Saviour Jesus Christ, Amen.

YEAR 2

If we endure, we shall reign with him.

Father, let your church be freshly inspired
to spread the gospel and serve the world
without thought of personal safety or comfort.
Silence for prayer
At all times and in all places:
you are our God

Father, raise up leaders in each community
who are honest and trustworthy,
and rekindle our enthusiasm
for honour and mutual respect.
Silence for prayer
At all times and in all places:
you are our God

Father, breathe into all our relationships
patience, understanding and affection,
keep marriages strong and friendships open-hearted.
Silence for prayer
At all times and in all places:
you are our God

Father, ease into wholeness the sick and the confused,
calm the fearful, soothe the sobbing,
unfasten the chained and let your love pour in.
Silence for prayer
At all times and in all places:
you are our God

Father, receive into your presence
the travellers who have come home to you,
and out of all evil and suffering bring good.

Silence for prayer

At all times and in all places:
you are our God

Father, may our praises and joyful thanks
be a sweet, fragrant offering at every part of our lives.

Silence for prayer

Merciful Father,
**accept these prayers
for the sake of your Son,
our Saviour Jesus Christ, Amen.**

21st Sunday
after Pentecost

YEAR 1

*In his own good time, God is drawing
all things to perfect completion.*

Father, deepen our awareness of your presence
in the moments and days, sorrows and joys,
and keep us ready and attentive.

Silence for prayer

Through time and eternity:
God is

Father, open the eyes of all leaders and their advisers
to seek wisdom, hold to what is right,
discern needs and care for the weak.

Silence for prayer

Through time and eternity:
God is

Father, be in our childhoods and our parenting,
be in our friendships, and those we shop
and work with.

Silence for prayer

Through time and eternity:
God is

Father, feed our needs, give us hope,
heal our sickness and bring us to lasting wholeness.

Silence for prayer

Through time and eternity:
God is

Father, walk with us through the journey of death,
welcome home those who have recently died
to this earthly life,
and cradle those who mourn in the comfort
of your arms.

Silence for prayer

Through time and eternity:
God is

Father, hear our thanks and praise
for your unchanging love pulsing always
under the activity of our lives.

Silence for prayer

Merciful Father,
accept these prayers
for the sake of your Son,
our Saviour Jesus Christ, Amen.

YEAR 2

*In his own good time, God is drawing
all things to perfect completion.*

Father, in all the decisions and activities of the church,
make us slow to rush ahead of you,
yet quick to follow where you lead.

Silence for prayer

We will not forget what you have done:
in you we put our trust

Father, in all areas of conflict and injustice,
keep us clear sighted, and attentive to your will.

Silence for prayer

We will not forget what you have done:
in you we put our trust

Father, with our friends, neighbours and loved ones,
with those we are tempted to despise,
give us opportunity to serve.

Silence for prayer

We will not forget what you have done:
in you we put our trust

Father, on those who are ill and frail,
place healing hands;
in those who live fearfully, breathe peace.

Silence for prayer

We will not forget what you have done:
in you we put our trust

Father, to the dead and dying bring rest;
to those who die unwanted and alone
give knowledge of their brothers' and sisters' concern.

Silence for prayer

We will not forget what you have done:
in you we put our trust

Father, with joy we call to mind your love,
and marvel at your affection for us.

Silence for prayer

Merciful Father,
accept these prayers
for the sake of your Son,
our Saviour Jesus Christ, Amen.

22nd Sunday after Pentecost

YEARS 1 AND 2

*You cannot live with self and God
both at the centre of your life; you will
have to choose between them.*

Father, take our faith and deepen it,
take our church and renew it,
take our need and supply it.
Silence for prayer
My God and my All:
let your kingdom come

Father, take our community and revitalise it,
take our government and guide it,
take our world and protect it.
Silence for prayer
My God and my All:
let your kingdom come

Father, take the young and empower them,
take the old and refresh them,
take the damaged and restore them.
Silence for prayer
My God and my All:
let your kingdom come

Father, take the suffering and comfort them,
take the frightened and reassure them,
take the lonely and befriend them.

Silence for prayer

My God and my All:
let your kingdom come

Take the dying and whisper peace to them,
take the dead and welcome them,
take the mourners and grieve with them.

Silence for prayer

My God and my All:
let your kingdom come

Take our minds and think through them,
take our mouths and speak through them,
take our lives and live through them.

Silence for prayer

Merciful Father,
accept these prayers
for the sake of your Son,
our Saviour Jesus Christ, Amen.

Last Sunday after Pentecost

YEARS 1 AND 2

Heaven is our home.

Father, look on your church and bless its work
in your name and power;
prune it and discipline it where necessary
and keep it safe from all evil.

Silence for prayer

Only in you, O Lord:
can we find rest

Father, look with mercy on this damaged,
ravaged world,
and bless the work to conserve and repair resources.

Silence for prayer

Only in you, O Lord:
can we find rest

Father, teach us to be good partners, friends,
parents, sons and daughters,
so that our behaviour reveals only your love.

Silence for prayer

Only in you, O Lord:
can we find rest

Father, we stand alongside the outcasts
and the mentally frail;
the disheartened, the angry and the vulnerable.
Silence for prayer
Only in you, O Lord:
can we find rest

Father, we stand alongside those who mourn
and those who die alone and unwanted.
Silence for prayer
Only in you, O Lord:
can we find rest

Father, we have known your peace and tranquillity
and want nothing more than to worship you
for ever.
Silence for prayer
Merciful Father,
accept these prayers
for the sake of your Son,
our Saviour Jesus Christ, Amen.